KABUKI
A Pocket Guide

(Frontispiece): Kinokuni-ya. Sawamura Sojuro III, from the series *Yakusha Butai no Sugata E*, by Toyokuni I, about 1795. Woodblock print. From the collection of the author.

KABUKI

A Pocket Guide

Ronald Cavaye

Photographs by Tomoko Ogawa

Tuttle Publishing
Boston • Rutland, Vermont • Tokyo

Published by Charles E. Tuttle Publishing,
an imprint of Periplus Editions (HK) Ltd.

LCC Card No. 92-63358
ISBN 0-8048-1730-8

First edition, 1993
First reprint, 1998

Printed in Singapore

Distributed by:
USA   Charles E. Tuttle Co., Inc.
      Airport Industrial Park
      RR1 Box 231-5
      North Clarendon, VT 05759
      Tel: (802) 773-8930
      Fax: (802) 773-6993

Japan Tuttle Shokai, Inc.
       1-21-13 Seki
       Tama-ku, Kawasaki-shi
       Kanagawa-ken 214, Japan
       Tel: (81) (44) 833-0225
       Fax: (81) (44) 822-0413

Southeast Asia
       Berkeley Books Pte Ltd.
       5 Little Road #08-01
       Singapore 536983
       Tel: (65) 280-3320
       Fax: (65) 280-6290

Tokyo Editorial Office:
2-6, Suido 1-chome,
Bunkyo-ku, Tokyo 112, Japan

Boston Editorial Office:
153 Milk Street, 5th Floor
Boston, MA 02109, USA

Singapore Editorial Office:
5 Little Road #08-01
Singapore 536983

To
my sadly missed
friends

MIZUTANI KENSUKE
and
MORI SHOJI
two great
kakegoe callers
who
so kindly
and
unreservedly
accepted me
into their world

Contents

List of Illustrations   9

Foreword *by Ichikawa Danshiro IV*   11

Preface   13

CHAPTER 1 : Kabuki—400 Years of History   17

CHAPTER 2 : Kabuki and Its Theater   22

CHAPTER 3 : The Plays   28

CHAPTER 4 : The Roles of the Actors   40

CHAPTER 5 : Stylized Acting   61

CHAPTER 6 : Music   74

CHAPTER 7 : Costumes, Wigs, and Makeup   80

CHAPTER 8 : Sets and Props   89

CHAPTER 9 : The Actors   96

CHAPTER 10 : The Audience   104

CHAPTER 11 : Backstage   127

CHAPTER 12 : At a Rehearsal   131

CHAPTER 13 : At a Performance   135

CHAPTER 14 : Where to See Kabuki   154

Appendix: List of Kabuki Actors   159

For Further Reading   163

Index of Actors, Plays, and Roles   167

Glossary-Index   171

List of Illustrations

(*) asterisks indicate color plates

(Frontispiece) Woodblock print by Toyokuni I of Sawamura Sojuro III   *page* 2

2. Noh stage   23
3. Woodblock print by Tsuruya Kokei of Ichikawa Danjuro XII   45
*4. Sukeroku and his lover   49
*5. Tomomori in *Yoshitsune Senbon Zakura*   50
*6. Onoe Kikugoro VII in *Tsuchigumo*   50–51
*7. Nakamura Kankuro V in *Kagami Jishi*   51
*8. Bando Tamasaburo V in *Sagi Musume*   52
*9. Onoe Kikugoro VII in *Benten Kozo*   53
*10. Izaemon and his lover in *Kuruwa Bunsho*   53
*11. Shizuka Gozen in *Yoshitsune Senbon Zakura*   54
*12. Nakamura Jakuemon IV as Hanako in *Musume Dojoji*   54–55
*13. Nakamura Utaemon VI as Masaoka in *Meiboku Sendai Hagi*   55
*14. Ichikawa Danjuro XII as Benkei in *Kanjincho*   56
15. Bando Yasosuke V applying *kumadori* makeup   85
16. *Oshiguma* of Ichikawa Sansho V (Danjuro X)   87
17. Modern Kabuki stage   91
18. Bando Mitsugoro IX in *Sanbaso*   105
19. Woodblock print by Toyokuni I of Nakamura-za theater   106–107
20. Ichikawa Danjuro XII in *Shibaraku*   108

21. Ichikawa Danjuro XII and Nakamura Jakuemon IV in *Narukami* 109
22. Onoe Baiko VII and Ichikawa Danjuro XII in *Kanadehon Chushingura* 110
23. Onoe Kikugoro VII and Onoe Kikuzo VI in *Kanadehon Chushingura* 110
24. Nakamura Kichiemon II in *Kumagai Jinya* 111
25. *Kotobuki Soga no Taimen* 112–113
26. Nakamura Fukusuke IX, Ichikawa Sadanji IV, and Nakamura Hashinosuke III in *Kuruma Biki* 114
27. Kataoka Nizaemon XIII and Ichimura Uzaemon XVII in *Terakoya* 115
28. Nakamura Shikan VII and Ichikawa Danjuro XII in *Kasane* 116
29. Nakamura Kankuro V and Matsumoto Koshiro IX in *Yotsuya Kaidan* 117
30. Bando Yasosuke V and Nakamura Tokizo V in *Naozamurai* 117
31. Nakamura Utaemon VI and Matsumoto Koshiro IX in *Seki no To* 118
32. Ichikawa Danjuro XII, Ichikawa Danshiro IV, and Nakamura Kankuro V in *Jiraiya no Danmari* 119
33. Ichikawa Danshiro IV and Ichikawa Kamejiro II in *Shinrei Yaguchi no Watashi* 120
34. Actors' crests 122–123
35. Ichikawa Danjuro XII and Onoe Kikugoro VII in *Kanjincho* 148–149

Foreword

by Ichikawa Danshiro IV

WHENEVER I perform abroad I am always surprised to meet Japanese people who have never seen Kabuki and know nothing about it. Often, however, they need only see Kabuki once to become completely fascinated by this unique theater.

My friend Ronald Cavaye has also been caught in Kabuki's ensnaring web. His love and involvement in Kabuki is so great that he has even become an *o-muko*, one of the *kakegoe* callers who shout out to the actors at important moments during the play and which are such a characteristic of Kabuki.

A real expert, in this book he introduces us to the foundations of Kabuki—its history and its actors, its acting styles and its performance, its color and its music—to the sheer beauty and joy of Kabuki.

As a Kabuki actor, I would like people to come to understand the heart of the Japanese people through this great art.

This book gives us a bridge—a *hanamichi* into the world of Kabuki.

Preface

KABUKI, the popular theater of Japan, began in about 1603 and is still flourishing today. It was the entertainment of the common people as opposed to Noh, the refined theater of the aristocracy, and is a close relative of the Bunraku puppet theater. All the actors in Kabuki, even those who play female roles, are men, and the plays and dances deal with the lives of the heroes and villains from Japan's real or legendary past.

Briefly, that is Kabuki. But such a description does not explain why foreigners will sit for four to five hours to see three or four often totally unconnected plays, understand not a word, and still come out of the theater saying it was "fantastic!" It does not explain why Greta Garbo, temporarily barred from the dressing room of Nakamura Utaemon VI, one of Kabuki's greatest *onnagata* (female-role actors), said, "I want to see his sweat!" and is reported to have said at the end of the performance that it was the most wonderful theatrical experience of her life. And it does not explain why this theater of the common people of feudal Japan still flourishes amidst the bustle of modern Tokyo and is appreciated and enjoyed throughout the world from Moscow to Minneapolis.

What is the secret of Kabuki? Why does it still speak to us who live in a world so unlike that which it portrays on the stage? Kabuki is often described as "The Resplendent Theater of Japan" or "Grand Kabuki," inviting comparison with Western opera. While it is true that the costumes and sets of some Kabuki plays, although by no means all, are really colorful and spectacular, these and the wild antics alone will not sustain the interest of the non-Japanese-speaking foreigner for hours on end.

I am not sure that even by the end of this book I will be able to answer my own question and explain the secret of Kabuki's attraction. Maybe there is no secret, or maybe its secret is its simplicity. Every country has its own theater, and perhaps we simply cannot resist, from the comfortable distance of our own armchairs or theater seats, watching the dramas and passions of others, whether they are portrayed in *Macbeth* or *Hamlet* or on television in a soap opera.

Kabuki is not difficult to understand. But it is, or can be, highly stylized, with its own rules and conventions. When a few of these conventions become clear, however, Kabuki can be great fun. It can be a bewildering experience to sit in the cheapest seats of the third floor of the Kabuki-za in Tokyo and be surrounded by the so-called *kakegoe* callers among the audience, whose shouts seem, at first anyway, to be more appropriate at a football game than in a theater. But when you have worked out just what to shout and when to shout it, the temptation to join in can be, as it was for me, irresistible.

I first saw a Kabuki play at the National Theater of Japan in Tokyo in 1979, and like several of my foreigner friends I became so fascinated by the music and drama of Kabuki and so impressed by the artistic standards of its actors that I suppose I must have been to the theater at least twice a week for seven years while living in Tokyo.

The idea of writing a book about Kabuki first occurred to me in about 1980. At that time the very successful English-language Earphone Guide commentaries at the Kabuki-za and National Theater had not yet come into operation, and without the help of a friendly expert, my only sources of information about Kabuki were books.

There are already many books in English about Kabuki, but I hope this one will fill the gap between those that are too technical, usually read only by theatrical scholars, and those that are glossy, often expensive books of photographs. I hope it will be useful for the first-time visitor who may only want to dip into it. At the same time I have tried to include enough detail to provide a comprehensive guide to the history, movement, dance, speech, and music that make Kabuki such unique theater.

All Japanese arts and sports have their own special vocabulary, and some words have no real English equivalent, or only a long-winded one. The walkway that runs from the main stage through the audience to the back of the theater, for example, is known as the *hanamichi,* but to refer to this in English by its literal meaning as the "flower-way" would be somewhat perverse. While I have tried to keep the number of Japanese words to a minimum, to learn a few of them is part of the fun of Kabuki, and I have always included the English equivalent or an explanation.

Japanese, especially written Japanese, is one of the most complex languages in the world. Its pronunciation, however, is not so difficult, and you will usually be understood if you give each syllable equal stress and pronounce the vowels as follows: *a* as in "father"; *e* as in "press"; *i* as in "Bali"; *o* as in "colt"; and *u* as in "true."

Consonants are usually paired with vowels: Ka-bu-ki; and when two consonants occur together they are usually pronounced as one. Tokyo, for example, is two syllables: To-kyo, not three as in To-ki-yo.

All names are given the Japanese way, surname first, and when an actor's name is given, either the complete name—Ichikawa Danjuro—or, as is the custom in Japan, only the forename—Danjuro—is used.

I give all direction from the point of view of the audience. "On the left" is therefore stage right, and "on the right" is stage left.

I would like to thank the many people who helped me with this book, particularly Honor Cooper, who read the manuscript after seeing Kabuki in London and who gave me many suggestions from a layman's point of view.

My thanks also go to the Kabuki management, Shochiku Co., Ltd., and in particular the chairman, Nagayama Takeomi, for allowing me access to the Kabuki-za over such a long period.

I must also thank the management, staff, and narrators of the Earphone Guide at the Kabuki-za, and in particular Kumon Ikuo, the president of the company Asahi Kaisetsu Jigyo, Ltd., and my friends Paul Griffith and Christopher Holmes. Their knowledge of Kabuki is quite extraordinary and they both gave me much valuable advice. I must especially thank Paul Griffith for checking the final draft of the manuscript.

Many Kabuki actors inspired me to write this book, and I would like, in particular, to mention Nakamura Utaemon VI, who has been a profound artistic inspiration to me, and to thank, as well, Ichikawa Ennosuke III, Bando Tamasaburo V, Matsumoto Koshiro IX, Nakamura Kankuro V, Nakamura Kichiemon II, and Onoe Baiko VII.

Finally, I would especially like to thank Ichikawa Danjuro XII for allowing us to use his photograph on the cover, and Ichikawa Danshiro IV, who so kindly wrote the foreword and who welcomed me so many times to his dressing room.

—Ronald Cavaye

London

CHAPTER 1

Kabuki
400 Years of History

 BEFORE THE seventeenth century, the principal forms of theater in Japan were the *bugaku* court dances, the aristocratic, refined Noh dramas with their accompanying Kyogen comedies, and the Ningyo Joruri, which developed into today's Bunraku puppet theater. The Noh drama had reached a state of perfection by the fourteenth century and was patronized by the daimyo (feudal lords) and the samurai upper classes. In Noh, the principal actors wear masks, and the dialogue, either chanted by the actors or by a small on-stage chorus, is accompanied by drums and a flute. Dance, which plays a major role in Noh, is slow and sedate, consisting of circular movements in which the feet rarely leave the floor except for an occasional rhythmic stamping. Props are kept to a minimum and the set is always the same: a pine tree painted on a plain wooden backdrop. The stage is small and characterized by a walkway extending from a greenroom to the main stage.

Puppets have been popular in Japan since the Heian period (794–1185), and the art of manipulating them has grown, together with developments in accompanying recitation and music. The three-stringed shamisen was introduced to Japan from China around 1560 and quickly rose in popularity. The chanted recitation accompanying the puppets was perfected by the great chanter Takemoto Gidayu (1651–1714), who founded a puppet theater in Osaka in 1685 and began a collaboration with Chikamatsu Monzaemon, widely regarded as Japan's greatest playwright.

The earliest reference to Kabuki dates to 1603 and a written record concerning a group of dancers led by a woman named Okuni. Okuni was probably a former shine maiden and possibly a prostitute. She and her group gave performances on a makeshift Noh stage set up on the dry bed of the Kamo River in Kyoto. Her dances, which did away with masks and were far livelier than anything seen in Noh, seem to have been an original mixture of folk dance and a type of religious dance called *nenbutsu odori*. They were supplemented with lewd skits concerning Nagoya Sanza (a famous samurai of the day), a courtesan or teahouse madam, and a clown. Okuni's dances and skits became extremely popular and the name Kabuki was applied to them, from the word *kabuku*, now archaic, which literally meant "titled" but implies that which is strange, exotic, and possibly somewhat risqué.

Okuni's Kabuki continued in this form for some years, becoming popular not only with the common people but also among the samurai and the feudal lords. Unfortunately, Kabuki also came increasingly under the scrutiny of the authorities, who regarded it as a disruptive influence. Eventually, in 1629, the Shogunate used the ever-present overtones of prostitution as an excuse to ban women from the stage on grounds of immorality. This ban lasted until the fall of the Shogun and restoration of the Emperor in 1868. Young dancing boys known as *wakashu* continued to perform the Kabuki dances, however. Though the boys, like the women, used the stage primarily to advertise their charms, they added acrobatics to the performances, and these are still an important feature of Kabuki. The boys were subjected to numerous rules, such as one requiring them to shave their forelocks, the presence of which was considered erotic in adult males. Although homosexuality was common, particularly among the upper classes, prostitution, both female and male, was not officially tolerated. In 1652, again on grounds of immorality, the young boys were also banned from the stage.

Kabuki, however, was allowed to continue, performed by mature males. As more emphasis was put on the text and mime, a higher level of drama developed, creating a need for more feminine roles. The art of the *onnagata*, the female-role player, was born. These female-role actors could not rely solely on their youth and physical beauty to carry the part, and so they emphasized and stylized feminine movements and gestures, thus creating the unique Kabuki women we see today. The dances, which had originally been the mainstay of Kabuki, also became increasingly the province of the *onnagata*.

With the mature male Kabuki, called *yaro kabuki*, we see the birth of the drama as we know it today. The primitive skits developed into mature plays, many of which were concerned with the *ukiyo* (the floating world), found in the licensed quarters of the cities. This is the world represented in *ukiyo-e*, the woodblock prints of courtesans, actors, and love-making. Permanent theaters were erected next to the pleasure quarters.

The new Kabuki repertoire also came under the influence of the older and traditional Noh dramas and Kyogen comedies as well as developing together with the puppet theater. The art of puppetry reached an artistic peak with the opening of Takemoto Gidayu's puppet theater in 1685. The combination of the so-called *gidayu* style of chanting or singing and Chikamatsu Monzaemon's plays became so popular that puppet dramas were quickly adapted by Kabuki actors. The two arts, although competing for the public's patronage, became very similar. In time the meaning of the word Kabuki changed and it came to be written with three characters: *ka*, meaning "song" and implying all music; *bu,* meaning "dance"; and *ki,* meaning "art or skill."

Thereafter, Kabuki developed greatly as an art. The first official playwright was listed in 1680, and star actors began to emerge. In the Kyoto-Osaka region, Sakata Tojuro I developed *wagoto,* an acting style for the realistic portrayal of young men in love. Meanwhile in Edo (present-day Tokyo) Ichikawa Danjuro I invented the bombastic style of acting called *aragoto,* which became enormously popular with the plebeian audience. Plays became more structured and were classified into dance pieces (*shosagoto*), history plays (*jidaimono*), and plays of the common people (*sewamono*). Remarkably, all this occurred within the narrow confines of the licensed quarters, in response to the artistic demands of the common people. Thus, it was their tastes and values that were reflected in the popular Kabuki dramas. At the same time, Kabuki continued to meet with the disapproval of the Shogunate, and plays and playhouses were subject to endless petty rules, regulations, and directives. In spite of these, Kabuki reached a state of artistic perfection from the seventeenth to the nineteenth centuries, becoming the most flourishing theatrical form in Japan.

In 1868, Kabuki along with the whole of Japanese society was rocked by the fall of the Shogunate and the opening of the country to the outside world. Now Japanese came to regard many of their own arts as culturally inferior to those of the West. Reflecting this mood of modern realism, the two greatest Kabuki actors of the day, Ichikawa Danjuro IX and Onoe Kikugoro V, introduced new plays to the repertoire. These plays did away with much of Kabuki's unique stylization. Fortunately, with one or two exceptions, the plays did not survive their originators. Nevertheless, these actors helped Kabuki to survive a difficult period, which in fact contributed to raising its formerly low status. In 1887, Emperor Meiji became Japan's first emperor to attend a Kabuki performance.

A further crisis occurred following World War II, when Kabuki was immediately censored by the Americans. The

Americans saw a glamorization of the feudal spirit in certain plays, and in light of recent events, considered this dangerous. A more enlightened approach was soon taken, however; the obvious artistic merits of Kabuki were recognized, and Kabuki was allowed to continue freely. In 1951, the Kabuki-za, destroyed in wartime firebombing, was reopened.

There is a tendency for people to idealize the past and pretend that things are not what they once were. Throughout this century there have been dire predictions that Kabuki as an art would not survive much longer. Kabuki was once the living theater of a plebeian audience clamoring almost weekly for new and exciting plays and innovations, and certainly it is no longer that today. There is a serious and valid argument that some plays are performed in far too earnest and sterile a manner and have lost the verve and vitality that once made them so popular. Nevertheless, the Kabuki we see now is still very much alive, flourishing in the hands of many fine actors, and is extraordinarily popular, drawing a large audience both in Japan and abroad. The theater of the Japanese commoner has, without a doubt, become one of the greatest theatrical art forms of the world.

CHAPTER 2

Kabuki and Its Theater

 TODO KABUKI can be seen in many different styles of theaters. It may be performed in theaters specially built for that purpose, such as Tokyo's Kabuki-za or the National Theater; or with a little adaptation, it can be staged in theaters and opera houses abroad, such as New York's Metropolitan. The principal feature of the Kabuki stage is the *hanamichi,* the extension that runs from the far left of the stage through the audience to a greenroom at the back of the theater. The word itself is almost international, and Sadler's Wells Theatre in London even possesses its own *hanamichi,* specially erected for Kabuki performances.

Unlike the Noh stage (Fig. 2), which has remained practically unchanged since its inception, the Kabuki playhouse has undergone five major developments.

The first occurred in the latter part of the seventeenth century with the addition of a draw-curtain *(hikimaku)* and the *hanamichi.* The origin of the *hanamichi* and even its name, "flower-way," are still the subject of much debate among scholars. One theory links

2. The Noh stage. The *hashigakari* walkway leads from the greenroom on the left to the main stage, which is about thirty meters square.

it to Noh and the three small steps leading from the auditorium to the front of the Noh stage. These steps were believed to have been used by the audience when presenting a favorite actor with *hana*, literally "flower," but meaning a gift, perhaps money. The Noh stage, however, has the *hashigakari*, which serves the same purpose as Kabuki's *hanamichi*. Thus it seems far more logical that the Kabuki *hanamichi* is simply the Noh *hashigakari* turned at ninety degrees.

The *hanamichi* brings the acting out from under the proscenium arch into the midst of the audience. Actors making their entrances along the sixty-foot *hanamichi* do so from the greenroom through a curtain called the *agemaku*. The *agemaku* plays a small but important role in an actor's performance. This curtain, decorated with the theater's crest, is hung from metal rings, which make a swishing sound on the rail when the curtain is drawn open or closed. An assistant employed to look after the small greenroom at the end of the *hanamichi* is also responsible for drawing back the *agemaku*. The way in which the curtain is opened clues the audience to the entering character—the louder the "swish," the more imposing the entrance.

The *hanamichi*, however, is more than just a means of making entrances and exits. It is also equipped with a lift called a *suppon*, used for supernatural appearances, at a point known as the *shichi-san*, the "seven-three." The *shichi-san*, seven-tenths of the way from the *agemaku* curtain and three-tenths from the main stage, marks the point of some of Kabuki's most important acting, and it is here that characters may stop to announce their names or to perform. Earlier, theater buildings were square in shape, and the seven-three point was turned around so that the actor stopped seven-tenths of the way from the main stage. With the appearance of Western-style, tiered theaters, this had to be reversed because the original position could not be seen from the theater's upper floors. Interestingly, however, Sukeroku, the hero of the play of the same name, still poses first at the original position when he makes his famous entry-dance.

Perhaps the greatest contribution of the *hanamichi*, however, is that it facilitates an intimate bond with the audience, something very difficult to achieve in a Western theater.

The addition of a draw-curtain across the main stage also proved a major innovation in Kabuki. In Noh, the main stage has no curtain at all, and the only curtain used in performances is located at the entrance to the *hashigakari* and is lifted by poles from the bottom corners.

The standard drop-curtain of the Western theater plays a static role, serving only to mark the beginning and ending of the play and the acts in between. In Kabuki, various curtains play more active roles, one curtain each at the beginning and end of a performance and several others during the play itself.

The most important of the Kabuki curtains is the *joshiki maku*, a light, billowy draw-curtain with broad green, terra cotta, and black stripes, opened from left to right. In modern theaters this stretches across the proscenium arch and has become the trademark of Kabuki. The three great theaters of Edo (Tokyo), the Nakamura-za, Ichimura-za, and Morita-za, are all said to have used tricolored striped curtains similar to the curtain seen today. Only the officially licensed theaters at that time were allowed to use such curtains. The *joshiki maku* is usually run open and closed at great speed for maximum effect. The one exception to this rule is the opening to the famous story of the forty-seven masterless samurai, *Kanadehon Chushingura.* The Japanese hold this story in such reverence that the curtain is opened very slowly, with great solemnity, taking about five minutes.

Occasionally a character may end a play from the *hanamichi,* as in Benkei's famous flying exit known as the *tobi roppo* at the end of *Kanjincho* (The Subscription Scroll). In this case, the musicians playing from the screened room, visible to the left of the stage, need to time their music to the actor's movements. Thus, the curtain is run across and held back so the musicians can see the actor as he stands on the *hanamichi.*

The next development of the theater occurred in the early part of the eighteenth century with the addition of a roof over the entire theater. Candles and panels near the roof, which could be opened and closed, helped to light the theater. In Noh, only the main stage was covered by a roof, and audiences were exposed to the elements. Performances were entirely dependent on the weather.

The end of the eighteenth century marked Kabuki's golden years when Kabuki truly came of age as a national art form. This period saw the flowering of the works of two of Kabuki's greatest writers, Tsuruya Nanboku (1755–1829) and later Kawatake Mokuami (1816–93), and the third major development in the theater, the appearance of the revolving stage, or *mawari-butai.* Although the revolving stage also appeared in Europe, its first continual use was in Japan, where its invention in 1758 is credited to Namiki Shozo. The *mawari-butai* allowed for very quick changes of scene and, in the early years, had two stages, one set within the other. The inside stage, called the *janome mawashi* (literally "snake's eye"), also made possible special effects such as boats sailing in opposite directions.

The theaters of this period had no seating, and the auditorium was divided by low bars into tatami-covered squares called *masu*. Each *masu* could comfortably accommodate about five people kneeling. (*Masu* can still be seen at Tokyo's Kokugikan stadium, the home of sumo.) Another important feature of the theaters of this period was the *kari hanamichi*, a second, slightly narrower *hanamichi* on the opposite side of the theater. The *kari hanamichi* was joined at the back of the auditorium to the main *hanamichi*, enabling actors to actually walk through and around the audience. Double entrances could also be made using both *hanamichi*. In today's theaters, the *kari hanamichi* is not always present and, if called for, must be specially erected.

The fourth change occurred during the Meiji era (1868–1912) with the introduction of gas and, later, electric lighting. Theaters were increasingly built using Western-style exterior architecture. The interiors, however, were still in the old style.

The fifth and final major development took place after the Great Kanto Earthquake of 1923 in which all the main theaters in Tokyo were destroyed. Many were rebuilt, doing away with *masu* and installing Western-style seating. The three great theaters of Edo, the Nakamura-za, Morita-za, and Ichimura-za, all faded away, the last, the Ichimura-za, being destroyed by fire in 1932. The Kabuki-za became the main Kabuki theater until it too was destroyed by the firebombing of World War II. It was rebuilt, however, and reopened in 1951. This was followed in 1966 by the opening of the new National Theater of Japan, the Kokuritsu Gekijo, which houses a large and small hall and is also the home of a Kabuki acting school.

Today it seems unlikely that the Kabuki theater will undergo any further changes, unless it is a reversion to an earlier stage. Already the modern lighting techniques and vastness of the modern theater have lessened the effect of certain Kabuki aspects, such as the broad-striped dramatic *kumadori* makeup.

There is now a large and growing movement dedicated to performing Kabuki in the few remaining premodern theaters, such as the enormously popular Kanamaru-za in the Shikoku region of Japan. One can only hope that it will not be long before a replica Edo-period theater will be built in Tokyo.

CHAPTER 3

The Plays

 KABUKI PLAYS are usually divided into three main categories: dances *(shosagoto)*, history plays *(jidaimono)*, and plays of the common people *(sewamono)*. Within these three categories are many subdivisions, and it is also quite common for the categories to overlap.

Shosagoto (dance)

Music and dance are the most important elements of Kabuki, as can be seen in the earliest mention of Kabuki, *kabuki odori* (Kabuki dances). Traditional Japanese dance, known as *buyo*, is fundamental to all Kabuki performance.

All Kabuki actors are to a greater or lesser degree dancers. They study dance from early childhood and continue formal lessons until they reach the age of about thirty. Even so, it is common for a very high-ranking dance teacher to supervise the rehearsals of even the most senior actors when performing in a dance.

Pure dances make up about one-third of the Kabuki repertoire. However, there are also many dance-dramas such as *Kanjincho* (The Subscription Scroll) (Figs. 14, 35) or *Funa Benkei* (Benkei in the Boat) in which long dance sections play a major role. Even in plays with no actual dancing, actors often adopt gestures and stances that reveal the influence of traditional dance. As Kabuki actors are trained in dance from such an early age, it is arguable whether they are ever entirely free of this influence.

Dance was an important element in early Japanese culture, and Kannami (1333–84) and his son Zeami (1364–1443) drew upon traditional dance forms when, toward the end of the fourteenth century, they brought the Noh theater to artistic fruition. The earliest Kabuki dances are believed to be based on the *nenbutsu odori,* which were once of a religious nature but later became influenced by secular folk dances. These early Kabuki dances were revuelike affairs in which women danced in a group. The rhythmic foot stamping, which is a feature of traditional Japanese dance, may have its origin in the dances' religious nature. The stamping was to call upon the gods and drive away evil spirits. In Kabuki, a special surface called *shosabutai* is laid on top of the main stage. This not only enhances the sound of the stamping but also provides a very smooth dancing surface.

The three basic elements of traditional dance are called *mai, odori,* and *furi. Mai* is the oldest style and is the term by which dance was known in Japan until the end of the fourteenth century. Literally meaning "to circle," *mai* is characterized by movements in which the feet for the most part remain in contact with the ground and the arms are moved in slow, graceful gestures. One of its features includes the walking style known as *suri-ashi,* in which the heels slide along the ground. *Mai* is the predominant dance style of Noh and therefore also is seen in Noh plays adapted to the Kabuki theater.

Odori is livelier and possibly has its roots in rhythmic folk dances. Although there may be a certain amount of movement through the air, leaps such as those seen in classical ballet are not performed in Japanese dance, and in general, as the knees are bent, the effect is to bring the whole body nearer to the ground.

Mime gestures, called *furi*, are also an important element of Kabuki dance which is always performed to songs rather than pure melody. Mime, such as the writing of a letter, the movement of waves, or falling petals, for example, are frequently employed to illustrate the song lyrics. Furthermore, objects such as fans or tenugui hand towels or even the sleeves of the kimono are often used to illustrate the actions in such mime. The fan, for example, can represent an arrow, a sakè cup, the moon, or, inverted, even Mount Fuji.

From 1652, dance became the province of the art of female-role specialists *(onnagata),* which developed rapidly from this date on. A major category of female dances was the so-called resentful spirit plays, or *onryogoto,* such as *Musume Dojoji* (The Maiden at Dojo Temple) (Fig. 12), in which a demure maiden turns into a serpent. Male dances became popular much later, with the emergence of dance-dramas such as *Seki no To* (Fig. 31), first performed by Nakamura Nakazo I (1736–90).

Kabuki dances developed to a state of great sophistication, with a variety of musical accompaniment. The art of making quick costume changes also developed to a high level and enabled one actor to perform several dances in quick succession. This genre of dance, called *hengemono,* or "transformation pieces," became very popular. Many of the dances we see today were originally part of a *hengemono.*

Quick costume changes meant that dances of considerable length could be choreographed without fear of losing the audience's attention. In the famous dance *Musume Dojoji,* which is over an hour long, the maiden changes costume nine times, twice in full view of the audience. This is done partially with the startling costume-change technique, *hikinuki,* in which threads of the special outer kimono are pulled out and the kimono comes apart to reveal a new kimono underneath. *Hikinuki* should not be confused with a similar technique known as *bukkaeri,* in which the upper half of the costume falls down over the lower, revealing a new pattern. *Bukkaeri* is used to symbolize the revelation of a character's true nature, whereas *hikinuki* is done purely for the visual spectacle.

A further major innovation in Kabuki dance occurred in the middle of the nineteenth century with the subtle and aesthetic integration of dance and drama derived from Noh. This began in 1840 when Ichikawa Danjuro VII, the most popular actor of the day, tried a daring experiment. He took a newly written adaption of the Noh play *Ataka* and performed it in Kabuki style. This was done in the face of considerable opposition from Noh actors and high-ranking officials, who resented this tampering by a common Kabuki actor, no matter how popular and wealthy. The play, which Danjuro called *Kanjincho* (The Subscription Scroll) was at first considered rather highbrow by the common-ers of Edo, but soon became one of the most popular of all Kabuki plays and gave rise to a whole new genre of plays adapted from Noh or the accompanying Kyogen comedies. Such pieces became known as *matsubame-mono.*

Matsu is Japanese for "pine," and *matsubame-mono* means roughly "pine-tree set." A huge, simple pine tree is painted on the backdrop and two angled side screens are decorated with a bamboo design. The right-hand screen has a small door set into it, corresponding to Noh's *kirido-guchi,* used for quick entrances and exits. The left-hand screen incorporates the grille behind which musicians play and (again from Noh) a brightly striped curtain raised by poles attached to the bottom corners. The main group of singers and musicians, dressed in formal costume, sit in full view of the audience on a tiered, scarlet platform in front of the pine-tree backdrop.

As in Noh or Kyogen, only simple props suggest the actual scene, and the audience must use its imagination. Although the musicians are on stage with the actors, they take no part in the actual drama and, like the puppeteers of the Bunraku puppet theater, quickly fade from the audience's attention.

Stylistic elements of Noh were also adopted with the plays. Most movements are slow, stately, and refined, and characters such as Togashi at the beginning of *Kanjincho* walk with the *suri-ashi,* heel-to-the-ground, sliding style of Noh plays. Although subtle Noh elements may be seen throughout the plays, they are without a doubt Kabuki, particularly the dance sections, which are far livelier than anything seen in Noh. *Matsubame-mono* tend, in fact, to be dance-dramas, and *Tsuchigumo* (The Earth Spider) (Fig. 6), *Migawari Zazen* (The Substitute), and *Suo Otoshi* (Dropping the Robe) are some of the most popular and appealing of all Kabuki plays.

Outside of Kabuki, the world of dance is divided into schools called *ryu,* each of which hands down its own particular dance traditions. Although several of the most important schools are actually headed by Kabuki actors, the schools are open to anyone. Thus, Japan's thriving dance world is only indirectly connected to Kabuki. Dance is one of the few elements of Kabuki that may still be regarded as a developing art in the sense that new dances are being choreographed and occasionally even performed on the Kabuki stage.

Jidaimono (history plays)

Jidai is Japanese for "era," and *mono* means "thing," thus *jidaimono* refers to a very broad range of plays dealing with samurai warriors and the upper classes, set in a period glamorized by Kabuki playwrights as a golden age of chivalry and heroism.

Jidaimono sets and costumes are spectacular, with characters dressed with a lavish opulence that would actually have been quite impractical in the real world. Movement on stage tends toward stiff formal posture; and the language of the drama, too, as befitting that of heroic and aristocratic character, is formal, elaborate, and difficult to understand, much like Shakespearean English is to the modern audience.

Many *jidaimono* are set in the late Heian (794–1185) and Kamakura (1185–1336) periods. Others are directly concerned with the Heike-Genji civil wars of the latter part of the twelfth century, which are documented in the famous *Heike Monogatari* (The Tale of the Heike). The Heike-Genji struggle proved such a popular theme of the puppet theater and Kabuki that stories were often set in that world in order to make them more exciting and romantic to the audience. Particularly popular were stories concerning the legendary Genji lord Yoshitsune. In fact, two of Kabuki's most famous plays, *Yoshitsune Senbon Zakura* (Yoshitsune and the Thousand Cherry Trees) (Figs. 5, 11) and *Kanjincho* are directly concerned with this story.

Another favorite Kabuki *sekai*, or "world," is the true story of the Soga brothers, Juro and Goro. In 1193, Soga Juro and his younger brother Goro successfully carried out a vendetta to avenge their father, who had been killed eighteen years earlier when they were children. Both brothers were killed in the vendetta, but their heroic deed fired the imagination of the people, much the same way as the forty-seven masterless samurai did in 1703, now immortalized in the great play *Kanadehon Chushingura.*

The Soga brothers' story was first recounted in a medieval tale called the *Soga Monogatari* (The Tale of the Soga Brothers) and, with the birth of Kabuki, the story was seen as ideal material with which to thrill the audience.

The brothers were elevated almost to the point of deification, and plays concerning them came to have an auspicious nature. By the time of Danjuro II (1688–1758) it had become the custom to perform a Soga play at the start of the new year. The most famous play directly concerning the brothers, *Kotobuki Soga no*

Taimen (The Auspicious Confrontation of the Soga Brothers) (Fig. 25), is still performed as a celebratory or congratulatory piece.

The brothers believe Lord Kudo Suketsune to be responsible for their father's death. Through the intervention of their friend Asahina, they are invited to a gathering at Kudo's mansion. Juro has difficulty restraining his impetuous younger brother from attacking Kudo. Kudo, in a show of contempt, throws the brothers two passes to a hunting party he is arranging near Mount Fuji. He implies that if they wish, they may attempt their vendetta there. The play ends at this point with a spectacular scene in which the characters strike a pose symbolizing a crane flying past Mount Fuji.

The practice of setting a story in a previous era, besides tending to glamorize the event, also served the more serious purpose of evading the censor. The Shogunate tried to impose strict controls over the people and the information available to them. Playwrights and actors who wished to dramatize a contemporary event escaped censorship by changing the names and setting the story in a previous era. The most famous example of this is the great classic play *Kanadehon Chushingura* (Figs. 22, 23). In 1703, forty-seven masterless samurai avenged the death of their lord by killing the lord who had caused his downfall, Kira Yoshinaka. The vendetta accomplished, they all committed *seppuku* (also known as *harakiri*)—ritual suicide by disembowelment. This heroic but, in the eyes of the government, dangerous act thrilled the people and was staged by Bunraku and Kabuki using an earlier time and different names. (Changing the vendetta leader's name from Oishi Kuranosuke to Oboshi Yuranosuke could have fooled no one, however.)

Famous *jidaimono* include the three great Kabuki classic plays of *Chushingura, Yoshitsune Senbon Zakura* (Yoshitsune and the Thousand Cherry Trees), and *Sugawara Denju Tenarai Kagami* (The Secret of Sugawara's Calligraphy) (Figs. 26, 27). Other famous examples are *Meiboku Sendai Hagi* (Fig. 13), *Shunkan*,

Moritsuna Jinya, Kumagai Jinya, and *Imoseyama Onna Teikin* (An Example of Noble Womanhood).

Sewamono (plays of the common people)

Sewamono plays deal with contemporary life in premodern Japan and utilize realistic sets, costumes, and speech. The acting is in general more natural, and the language is closer to modern Japanese. Sets commonly show a typical house of the period, sometimes surrounded by a small yard or garden. Entering by way of a gate on the left, characters climb one or two steps to a cutaway room which is usually raised about a meter higher than the main stage. In contrast to the gorgeous costumes of *jidaimono*, clothing, makeup, and hair tend toward the actual styles of the time (Fig. 30).

Sewamono have their roots in the type of play most popular in the Kyoto–Osaka region, where the more natural style of acting called *wagoto* was favored. The first real *sewamono* play is said to have been one of the many stories surrounding the courtesan Yugiri and her lover Izaemon, ending tragically with the double suicide of the pair. The best of the many plays concerned with this story is *Kuruwa Bunsho* (Love Letters from the Licensed Quarter), which was written in 1679 by the great playwright Chikamatsu Monzaemon. Monzaemon (1653–1724) wrote plays for both Kabuki and Bunraku, including many history plays. His *sewamono*, however, are his most prized plays today, *Sonezaki Shinju* (Love Suicide at Sonezaki) and *Koi Bikyaku Yamato Orai* (Love's Courier on the Yamato Highway) being fine examples which are often performed.

Sewamono are basically concerned with the lives of the townspeople and merchants, those who largely made up the Kabuki audience of the time. Under the yoke of oppressive government restrictions, the conflict between duty *(giri)* and emotion *(ninjo)* figures largely in many Kabuki plays. *Sewamono* often depict the tragic consequences of a character following his heart instead of the path of duty. This often led to suicide, in particular, double suicide *(shinju)*, in which the frustrated couple decide to end their lives in the hope of meeting again in the next world. Such plays were very popular, and real *shinju* became so common that the government actually tried to prohibit it.

In *sewamono*, great attention is paid to small details of everyday life, and in many respects these plays are an accurate mirror of premodern Japanese society. Such actions as the lighting of a pipe, the preparation of food, or the application of makeup are often depicted with a fine degree of realism. Actors take great pride in their performance of these details, handing their skills down from generation to generation. (These skills, called *kata*, are dealt with in more detail on p. 71)

It is possible to subdivide *sewamono* plays according to area and subject matter. Plays about thieves became popular, possibly because the life of a thief was seen as a justifiable rebellion against a repressive society. Such plays are called *shiranami-mono*, or "white-wave plays," after the name of an infamous group of bandits. The most famous *shiranami-mono* is *Benten Kozo* (Benten the Thief) (Fig. 9), which was written by Kawatake Mokuami in 1862 and is frequently performed today.

Ghost plays, or *kaidan-mono*, constitute another category, the finest of which is the story of the poisoned Oiwa who comes back to haunt her husband in *Yotsuya Kaidan* (Fig. 29). As a result of the curse of Oiwa and the many accidents that have actually occurred during performances of this play, actors make it a practice to visit Oiwa's shrine in Tokyo's Yotsuya to pray for her soul before the beginning of a theater run.

Although *sewamono* may not at first appear as visually attractive and splendid as some *jidaimono*, stylization is just as important. Such devices as stylized posing and rhythmic speech are frequently employed. As with many other aspects of Kabuki, the lines between acting styles and types of plays are often blurred, and it is quite common to find elements of *sewamono* within *jidaimono* and vice versa. Kanpei's *seppuku* in Act VI of *Chushingura*, for example, is in typical, realistic *sewamono* style, though the whole play is classified as *jidaimono* and set in an earlier era.

There are two further subcategories of plays that are important enough to deserve special mention: the *danmari* and the special collection of eighteen plays known as the Juhachiban.

Danmari (pantomime)

A *danmari* is a pantomime accompanied by rather slow, languorous music. A group of characters grope around the stage in what is supposed to be total darkness, trying to find some precious object. The characters, with stylized graceful movements, bump into and circle one another, alternately gaining possession of and then losing the object they are trying to get hold of. They form picturesque groups, climaxing in stop-motion poses called *mie*, and eventually, as dawn breaks or the moon comes out from behind the clouds, the main character will emerge triumphant over the others with the amulet, scroll, letter, or whatever the sought-after object may be.

There are two basic types of *danmari*: the historical or *jidai danmari*, which is a short, separate play in its own right; and the domestic or *sewa danmari*, which is one short section of a longer play.

Originally, *jidai danmari* were performed as part of the *kaomise*, or "face-showing," performances at the beginning of the theater year in November, when newly engaged actors were introduced to the audience. To show off the actors in the best possible light, the *danmari* was made as spectacular as possible, with gorgeous costumes and special effects, such as quick changes and dramatic stylized exits known as *roppo*. *Miyajima no Danmari* (Danmari at Miyajima) and *Jiraiya no Danmari (Fig. 32)* are examples of *jidai danmari* still performed today.

The best example of a *sewa danmari* occurs in *Yotsuya Kaidan*.

Oiwa and a young man named Kohei have been murdered by Iemon, Oiwa's husband. The bodies of both Oiwa and Kohei are washed up on a canal bank and begin to haunt Iemon. At the end of this scene, various other characters emerge in the darkness and break into a *danmari* as they search for a scroll containing the names of vendetta conspirators, which is a subplot to the play.

Juhachiban (The Eighteen Plays)

The collection of plays known as the Juhachiban holds a special place in Kabuki history, and the performance of one of them is regarded as a special event even today.

In March 1840 at the Kawarazaki-za in Edo, Ichikawa Danjuro VII performed *Kanjincho* for the first time. The play was advertised as *Juhachiban no Uchi* (From the Eighteen), and was the first of a collection by Danjuro of the best and most popular plays in his acting style.

Which plays were actually included in this collection has been a matter of much research. One of the plays, *Oshimodoshi* (Devil Pusher), is no longer performed as a play at all but is a character seen most frequently in the alternative ending to the dance *Musume Dojoji*. Danjuro VII (1791–1859) adopted these plays as his *ie no gei*, or "family art." Though they may be performed by other actors, they are now considered the speciality of Danjuro XII. Later, other actors such as Onoe Kikugoro V (1844–1903) and Ichikawa Enno I (1888–1963) followed Danjuro's example and adopted particular plays as their speciality.

Several of the Juhachiban are among the most popular and well-known plays in the Kabuki repertoire. Representative of Danjuro's art, they are either done totally in the bombastic style of acting known as *aragoto,* or, as in the case of *Kanjincho*, have elements of *aragoto* in them. After *Kanjincho*, the most popular, mature, and extended is *Sukeroku Yukari no Edo Zakura* (Sukeroku and the Cherry Blossoms of Edo), in which Sukeroku (Fig. 4) (actually Soga Goro) pursues the vendetta to avenge his murdered father.

As an example of pure *aragoto* style, *Shibaraku* (Wait!) (Fig. 20) is the most celebrated play in Kabuki, and takes its name from the hero's shouts of *"Shibaraku! Shibaraku!"* (Wait! Wait!) as he enters to save a group of nobles from being beheaded.

Ya no Ne (The Arrowhead) is another piece of *aragoto* spectacle, with Soga Goro sharpening a gigantic arrow. Soga Goro also appears in *Uiro Uri,* disguised as a fast-talking medicine seller.

Kenuki (The Tweezers) shows Kumadera Danjo solving the mysterious illness of a princess whose hair stands on end (her hair ornaments are attracted by a magnet in the ceiling), and *Narukami* (Fig. 21) deals with the seduction of the priest Narukami by Princess Taema to release the imprisoned Dragon God of Rain.

Kagekiyo shows us Kagekiyo breaking out of his imprisonment and routing his captors in typical *aragoto* style.

The remainder of the Juhachiban are very rarely performed, although the National Theater in Tokyo has pursued a policy of reviving them. They are: *Fuwa,* an old story of a confrontation scene; *Zobiki,* a humorous story in which two *aragoto* characters have a tug of war with an elephant; *Nanatsumen,* about a mask maker; *Kamahige,* bombastic shaving with a sickle; *Fudo,* the Buddhist god and deity of the Ichikawa acting family; *Kan'u,* the story of a Chinese general; *Gedatsu,* another story about Kagekiyo and a gigantic bell; *Uwanari* (Jealousy); and *Jayanagi,* which deals with possession by an evil snake spirit.

The Juhachiban vary greatly in their level of quality. Few reach the level of the masterpiece *Kanjincho,* and many of the plays have now fallen into neglect. Despite being somewhat facile, Danjuro's plays shed much light on the *aragoto* style and reflect the tastes and values of the people of Edo.

CHAPTER **4**

The Roles of the Actors

IN THE EARLY days of Okuni's Kabuki, the first standard roles in the primitive skits, too short to be called real plays, were simply a man, a woman, and a clown. The male roles were also played by women.

With the banning of both women's and young boys' Kabuki and the development of a more mature type of theater, standards began to rise and art took precedence over the physical charms of the actresses and actors. Roles also developed and role-types became clearly defined. Certain actors became specialists, not only in male or female roles but also in subcategories such as old men, evil aristocrats, or young lovers.

Although some actors today perform both male and female roles, they usually specialize in either one or the other, the principal role-types being female roles called *onnagata* and male roles known as *tachiyaku*. Several Kabuki plays also have very substantial, important roles for children, so the son of a major actor will make his debut in a *koyaku* or child role.

Onnagata (female-role actors)

Female roles played exclusively by male actors are one of the most important features of Kabuki. First-time visitors to Kabuki often find it incredible that the beautiful young girl on stage is actually a man, maybe even a grandfather in his seventies.

From 1652, a government order declared that Kabuki could be performed only by mature male actors. As the actors aged, they sought to increase their on-stage beauty and femininity by exaggerating and stylizing female traits and movements. These became the art of *onnagata* that we see today. (*Onna* means "woman," *otoko* is "man," and *gata* roughly means "type.") To assure the authorities that women were not appearing on the stage, the actors playing these roles were required to register in advance. Thus, certain players became typecast as *onnagata*, as opposed to *otokogata*—or *tachiyaku* as they are called today—actors who performed exclusively male roles.

From these beginnings, female impersonation gradually developed into an art that was no longer an attempt to represent a real woman. Naturalism gave way to exaggeration and a forced but refined femininity. The voice is pitched in a high falsetto, and hand and arm movements, already constrained by the sleeves of the kimono, are small and tightly controlled. The shoulders droop, knees are bent to reduce height, and most noticeable of all, the walk becomes a tiny, feminine gait with knees held together and toes pointed inward. Even today, young actors at Tokyo's National Theater School practice walking with a sheet of paper between their knees.

Within the broad *onnagata* category there are many subcategories depending on age, character, and social status. Even a simple bow of greeting can be quite different depending on whether it is done by a princess *(hime-sama)*, a town girl *(machi musume)*, or a middle-aged woman. The *hime-sama* role is one of the most interesting. Since the actors and authors of Kabuki plays had never seen a real princess, an entirely imaginary character was invented. Often refined to the point of immobility, she is usually dressed in a scarlet kimono with a silver tiara and sits on folded knees with her right hand demurely held across her breast and her left hand extended in the kimono sleeve to her side. "Pins and needles princess" *(shibire hime)* is the name often given to these roles because of the obvious discomfort involved in retaining the position for long.

Perhaps the finest, and certainly the most spectacular, of the *onnagata* roles is the high-ranking courtesan type called *oiran,* such as Agemaki from the play *Sukeroku.* Her kimono and outer robes are gorgeous and her hair is highly decorated with many pins and ornaments. *Oiran* tend to be rather monumental, static figures whose favors were not easily obtained. They are a rare example of female dominance in the aggressive masculine society of Japan.

With the Meiji era came the new mood of realism and calls to allow women back into Kabuki. Fortunately, however, it was too late. The stylization was complete and the *onnagata* had become a separate theatrical entity. Were women to perform Kabuki today they would no doubt appear far too natural and would need to adopt the stylized "masculine" femininity necessary as a real Kabuki *onnagata.* The falsetto voices of the male actors, for example, so strange when first heard, soon become an integral part of a Kabuki performance, and a real female voice lacks the hard edge that characterizes the role of the *onnagata.*

One of the most important points of the *onnagata* art is that the stylization employed to perform a role, the result of many years of subtle refinement by great actors of the past, means that it is possible for any actor of any age to perform a role and be perfectly convincing. Once the convention has been accepted by the audience, real age becomes unimportant, and the twenty-year-old maiden on stage may well be, and very often is, played by an actor in his seventies or older.

Tachiyaku (male-role actors)

Players of male roles are generally called *tachiyaku*. Like *onnagata*, male roles can be divided into categories, depending on age and social status. In general, actors are capable of performing any type of role by simply adopting certain stylized acting techniques. In practice, however, an actor's physical attributes can lead to his becoming typecast. The naturally deep voice of Ichikawa Sadanji IV, for example, precludes his playing young men, and Sukedakaya Kodenji II (born 1909) actually performed old men from his youth.

The two most important male-role types are the bombastic superheroes of the *aragoto* style popular with the commoners of Edo, and the refined young lovers performed in the "gentle" *wagoto* style, which was preferred in the Kyoto-Osaka region.

Aragoto

"Shibaraku! Shibaraku!" (Wait! Wait!) shouts Kamakura Gongoro as the evil Takehira is about to have the young Lord Yoshitsuna and his followers beheaded. As Takehira's retainers quake at the sound of this fearsome voice, from the back of the theater Gongoro enters along the *hanamichi* in one of the most spectacular costumes in the history of the theater.

Gongoro, in the play *Shibaraku,* is a superhero performed in the acting style of enormous exaggeration in costume, makeup, movement, and vocal delivery known as *aragoto*. His face is painted with broad stripes of red and black, and the sidelocks of his hair stick out like the spokes of a wheel. The topknot of his wig is tied with the winglike paper bow called *chikara-gami* which signifies strength, and the crown of the wig is unshaven. The unshaven crown signals that for all his fearsome qualities Gongoro is still but a youth. His costume is so enormous that the actor has difficulty walking. Long trailing trousers, known as *naga-bakama*, hide fifteen-centimeter-high clogs. Vast meter-

and-a-half-square sleeves imprinted with the Ichikawa family crest are held up and supported by bamboo struts. Later in the play Gongoro decapitates several men with one blow of his two-meter-long sword. (Fig. 3)

Aragoto, the most outlandish of Kabuki's acting styles, was founded by Ichikawa Danjuro I (1660–1704), who was regarded as the most popular actor in Edo. *Aragoto* is actually a shortened form of *aramushagoto,* meaning "wild-warrior style," and Danjuro is said to have based his acting on a violent warrior puppet character called Kinpira, who was extremely popular with the plebeian audience of the time. To complement the wild antics of the puppet, Danjuro invented exaggerated movement and fantastic costumes, and painted his face with broad stripes of makeup called *kumadori.* To reflect his appearance he employed a forceful and exaggerated style of vocal delivery. At the end of *Shibaraku,* for example, Gongoro goes off shouting *"Yat'toko tot'tcha, un toko na!"* a nonsense phrase designed merely to complement his appearance and strike fear in his enemies. The stop-motion, cross-eyed poses known as *mie,* which serve to stress important moments in the play, may have been inspired by Buddhist statuary, whose fierce expressions are intended to ward off evil. Danjuro worshiped the god Fudo Myoo, and certain of his *mie* poses were performed as Fudo Myoo is usually depicted—holding a rope in one hand with which he binds and hauls souls to their salvation, and in the other a sword with which he severs them from carnal desire.

This bombast proved so popular, especially in Edo, that Danjuro adopted it as his family art, or *ie no gei.* The *aragoto* style was further refined by his son Danjuro II; and later, in the nineteenth century, when Danjuro VII made his collection of favorite plays, the Juhachiban, all the plays with the exception of *Kanjincho* were in the *aragoto* style. *Aragoto* is regarded as the property of the Ichikawa family, and although *aragoto* roles may be performed by other actors, they remain the speciality of the present holder of the name, Danjuro XII.

3. Ichikawa Danjuro XII as Kamakura Gongoro in *Shibaraku,* by Tsuruya Kokei, 1985. Woodblock print. From the collection of the author.

Although some roles such as Gongoro are played in the pure *aragoto* style, other roles are sometimes performed with a mix of styles, resulting in a more realistic manner. Sukeroku, for example, in the play of the same name, is not a pure *aragoto* character, and both his appearance and movements, particularly during his dance of entry on the *hanamichi,* show elements of the refined style of *wagoto.* Benkei, too, the hero of *Kanjincho,* cannot be regarded as pure *aragoto,* although he does perform some *aragoto* techniques such as *mie* poses and the *tobi roppo,* his famous bounding exit at the end of the play.

Wagoto

From the birth of Kabuki and for the next two hundred and fifty years, until 1868, Kyoto was the capital of Japan. The Kyoto area and the nearby city of Osaka were considered the commercial and cultural center of the country. The ruling Shogunate, however, had established itself in the east in what had been the tiny fishing village of Edo. As a result, Edo rapidly developed into a major city.

The audience of the Kyoto-Osaka region, however, considered itself to be more sophisticated and refined than that of Edo. Though the histrionics of Edo's *aragoto* were occasionally enjoyed, the preferred style was a gentler, more realistic one. The region's most famous actor, Sakata Tojuro I (1647–1709), is credited with the development and perfection of the gentle style known as *wagoto*.

Wagoto is a comparatively realistic style of acting for a male role and is generally employed in the portrayal of a young lover. The face is painted white to indicate youth. The hair, in sharp contrast to the exotic wigs of *aragoto,* is styled in the standard topknot, and the crown of the head is shaven, the fashion for all men in premodern Japan. The voice is natural, though high-pitched, again to indicate youth, and movements are gentle and refined. *Wagoto* characters avoid heavy masculine gestures and even walk with a slightly feminine gait. Another important element of *wagoto* is the faint air of comedy. Young men in love are portrayed as somewhat silly, and despite often strained circumstances, there is an emphasis on the comic side of their situations.

The most famous play featuring a *wagoto* character is *Kuruwa Bunsho,* also known as *Yoshidaya* (Fig. 10), the name of the teahouse in which it is set. Many of the earliest Kabuki skits were concerned with the social niceties of obtaining a courtesan, a process that fascinated the common people, who, because of the great expense involved, could only dream of such a situation. There were many ranks of prostitutes, of which the highest was the courtesan known as the *keisei* or *oiran.* Treated as a queen, she could not be purchased, and a client was accepted only if he pleased her with his wit and manners. The depiction of winning over an *oiran* was called *keisei-kai*, "courtesan buying."

There was a famous scandal involving a courtesan named Yugiri and her penniless lover, Izaemon, in which the pair eventually committed double suicide. As was the custom, this story was quickly reenacted on the stage in many variations, of which the most famous, and the only one regularly performed today, is *Kuruwa Bunsho*. The story is a simple one in which Izaemon, disinherited because of his squandering in the licensed quarters and relationship with Yugiri, returns to the teahouse dressed in a paper kimono stitched together from Yugiri's love letters. Izaemon is welcomed as a once-valued customer and nervously and comically awaits Yugiri's entrance. Yugiri is splendidly attired, as a courtesan of the first rank; and pining for her lover, whom she believes to have left her for another, she wears a purple headband knotted on the left, a Kabuki convention indicating illness. The couple is reconciled and in the end the joyous news is brought that Izaemon's family has relented and he is wealthy once more. The play's charm lies in the ambience of the teahouse atmosphere at the New Year and the love scene between Yugiri and Izaemon, played in a coquettish, typical *wagoto* style.

Apart from *aragoto* and *wagoto* characters, other male roles may be subdivided into four main role-types, each of which has a number of subclassifications.

Villains (*kataki-yaku*) are made up of three groups: the evil aristocrats (*kuge-aku*), the "red-face" characters (*akattsura*), and the evil samurai (*jitsu-aku*). *Kuge-aku* tend to be rather imposing characters such as Takehira in *Shibaraku*. He wears the formal robes of a high-ranking aristocrat and an exaggerated wig with huge manelike sidelocks. His face is painted with the bold lines of *kumadori* makeup, although the color, unlike the red used for the hero of the play, is blue, indicating his cold-blooded nature. *Kuge-aku* may also have an aura of magical power. Shihei, for example, in *Kuruma Biki* subdues the brothers Umeomaru and Sakuramaru with nothing more than a menacing glance.

The red-faced *akattsura* characters are lower on the social scale than the *kuge-aku* and are often seen as messengers or envoys. Although they may have some form a *kumadori* make-up, the reason for their name is that the makeup base is red as opposed to white or flesh tone. Genba, who comes to collect the head of the young boy Kan Shusai in the *"Terakoya"* (The Village School) act from the classic play *Sugawara Denju Tenarai Kagami*, is a typical *akattsura* character.

Evil samurai are referred to as *jitsu-aku* and are less obviously malevolent than the *kuge-aku* or *akattsura*, although a close study of their wigs and makeup may reveal subtle deviations as indications of the characters' true natures. Their makeup may include patches of facial shadow as opposed to the pure white of other aristocratic characters, and the wig may have stylized dishevelment around the topknot or sides.

Although *wagoto* is used to portray somewhat foolish young men in love, the general term for young, rather refined men is *nimaime*, which means literally "second flat thing." This comes from the time when actors were advertised on boards outside the theater and the actors who played these roles occupied the second row. (These boards can still be seen outside the Minami-za theater in Kyoto during the December *kaomise*, or "face-showing" performances. The old segregation of actors into role types, however, is no longer practiced.) A *nimaime* role is characterized by a pure white face and high-pitched voice, both of which indicate youth and high breeding. Movements and walk are refined and almost feminine. Because actors naturally tend toward either female or aggressive masculine roles, *nimaime* is actually the rarest type of Kabuki actor.

The third major category of male roles is the clowns, called *doke-gata* or *sanmaime*, "third flat thing," as they occupied the third row of boards. One of the finest clown roles is that of Banni, the stupid retainer of Ko no Morano, the villain of *Kanadehon Chushingura*.

The final role type is that of the old man, and as this is a

4. *Sukeroku.* Sukeroku and his lover, the courtesan Agemaki. Sukeroku,
Ichikawa Danjuro XII. Agemaki, Nakamura Jakuemon IV.

5. *Yoshitsune Senbon Zakura*, Act III. Tomomori kills himself by tying the rope of an anchor around his waist and casting it into the sea. Tomomori, Ichikawa Danjuro XII.

6. *Tsuchigumo.* The earth spider weaves its enormous web around the warriors. The spider, Onoe Kikugoro VII.

7. *Kagami Jishi*. The roles of the young girl Yayoi and the lion are danced by the same actor. Here, the lion, played by Nakamura Kankuro V, is teased by two butterflies, played by his sons, Nakamura Kantaro II and Nakamura Shichinosuke II.

8. *Sagi Musume.* The spirit of the heron maiden is danced by Bando Tamasaburo V.

9. *Benten Kozo.* The thief Benten Kozo, dressed as a girl, reveals his tattooed shoulder and his true identity. Benten Kozo, Onoe Kikugoro VII.

10. *Kuruwa Bunsho.* Izaemon and his lover Yugiri pose happily together at the end of the play. Izaemon, Nakamura Ganjiro III. Yugiri, Onoe Baiko VII.

11. *Yoshitsune Senbon Zakura*, Act VI. Shizuka Gozen travels to meet her lover Yoshitsune accompanied by Tadanobu, who is actually a fox. Shizuka, Nakamura Jakuemon IV. Tadanobu, Ichikawa Ennosuke III.

12. *Musume Dojoji*. The dancer Hanako reveals herself as a serpent and mounts the bell that kept her lover from her grasp. The serpent, Nakamura Jakuemon IV.

13. *Meiboku Sendai Hagi.* Masaoka pours out her grief over the body of her murdered son. Masaoka, Nakamura Utaemon VI.

14. *Kanjincho*. Benkei poses before his jubilant *tobi roppo* bounding exit. Benkei, Ichikawa Danjuro XII.

somewhat general category, elements of other styles may also be included. The role of Ikyu, for example, in *Sukeroku* is really a cross between a *kuge-aku* and *jitsu-aku*. Old townsmen are often seen in plays of the common people *(sewamono)*, and there are many fine "father" roles such as Shirataya from Act III of *Sugawara Denju Tenarai Kagami* and Magoemon from the *"Nino-kuchi Mura"* (Ninokuchi Village) act of *Koi Bikyaku Yamato Orai.*

Seppuku (ritual suicide)

Before leaving this section on male roles, I would like to explain a little about the practice of ritual suicide *(seppuku* or *harakiri)* which plays an important part in many Kabuki plays. Although by no means are all Kabuki plays concerned with this subject, ritual suicide is still widely misunderstood in the West.

The word *seppuku* is a polite reading of the characters for what is known (and usually mispronounced) in the West as *harakiri. Hara* means "belly" and *kiri* is from *kiru,* meaning "to cut." In this case, *hara* indicates far more than a mere body part. It is considered the bodily abode of the soul and the center of all thought and emotion. The children of the samurai class were taught from an early age not to fear death, and that one day they might have to take their own lives in this way.

Kabuki's most celebrated and formal *seppuku* comes from *Kanadehon Chushingura* (Fig. 22), in which Lord Enya Hangan is ordered to commit suicide for the capital offense of drawing his sword in the Shogun's palace. With great formality, two tatami mats are first laid out bottom-side up and covered with a white cloth. Small sprigs of green *shikimi* plant are placed in stands at each corner. Hangan, dressed in the pale, off-white clothes of death, kneels on the mats and draws the shoulder wings of his formal clothes tightly under his knees. The etiquette of *seppuku* dictates that the wound not be exposed after death, and the taut cloth will pull his body forward as he dies. He wraps paper around the upper part of the dagger so that he can grip it with both hands and, feeling for the bottom of his rib cage, plunges the dagger into his left abdomen. He then draws the knife across to the right and makes a final small upward cut. *Seppuku* is a slow, agonizing death, and to dispatch himself he withdraws the dagger and cuts his jugular vein.

Within the same play there is an interesting contrast when one of Hangan's retainers, Kanpei, also commits *seppuku* in Act VI (Fig. 23). He is living in the country and wishes to take part in the vendetta. However, he is led to believe that he has inadvertently killed his own father-in-law. Almost on the spur of the moment, in contrast to the formality of Hangan's preparations, he plunges his short sword into his stomach. Kanpei, too, cuts his own jugular vein. Actually, it was more common to have an assistant, often a friend, known as a *kaishaku*, behead the victim at a prearranged point during the suicide. Timing was important because a simple execution was considered a disgrace. The initial cut had to be made by the victim himself. Compassion, however, could in some cases lead to the blow being struck almost as soon as the first cut had been made, and honor satisfied.

Despite its dramatization of the act, Kabuki must have played a large part in educating the common people in the way of Bushido, the code of the warrior, in feudal Japan.

Koyaku (child roles)

As Kabuki is an art handed down through generations, the children of star actors tend to make their stage debut at a very early age.

Child roles, *koyaku*, which may be parts of quite considerable length and complexity, may be given to children as young as eight or nine years old. Because of the great importance attached to succession in Kabuki, the children of ranking actors are expected to follow in their fathers' footsteps and make their debuts at the age of five or six.

Children of even three or four may be introduced to the stage, as in the case of Nakamura Kantaro II, the first grandchild of the late Nakamura Kanzaburo XVII. He first appeared on the stage hand-in-hand with his grandfather, as one of the many priests who enter at the beginning of the famous dance *Musume Dojoji.* Occasionally, special performances may be staged for one or two days in which the children take the main roles of a play such as the "Mustering Scene" from *Benten Kozo* (Benten the Thief), where the gang of five thieves, elegantly dressed holding umbrellas, are accosted by the police. Young children of ranking actors sometimes take these roles with their fathers acting as the black-dressed stage assistants called *kurogo.* The performances are greatly enjoyed by the audience.

Koyaku are similar to adult roles in all but one important respect. All children in Kabuki speak in a high-pitched monotone. The reasoning behind the tradition is unclear, but this manner of speech is highly distinctive and, as children in Kabuki plays are often tragic victims, it can be extremely expressive.

When children perform in a proper Kabuki run they appear every day for the month, their schooling fitted in around the performance. Most will share a dressing room with their father, although minor roles, such as the children who taunt the poor demented girl Onatsu in the dance *Onatsu Kyoran,* for example, will be accommodated with the adult supporting-role players. As in the case of the adults, child actors for such roles may not come from Kabuki families. They are drawn from several schools with a connection to the theater and given special training. It is also common for minor roles to be given to girls as well as boys. This is the only time females may be seen on the Kabuki stage.

Some famous examples in which children play a major role are Act III from *Meiboku Sendai Hagi* in which Senmatsu, the child of the lady-in-waiting, Masaoka, sacrifices himself to save his young lord by deliberately eating poisoned cakes; and the play *Yamanba,* about the old woman of the mountains and her grandson of fabulous strength, Kaidomaru. Children may also dance the parts of the two butterflies appearing in the middle of *Kagami Jishi*, Kabuki's most famous lion dance.

Traditionally, children of Kabuki actors had no choice but to follow their fathers into the profession. However, certain actors today are not so strict in this respect and allow their sons to wait and make the decision for themselves when they are older. The system is without doubt very hard on the children of Kabuki actors as well as being unfair to those not born within the Kabuki world. As with similar Western arts, excellence may be achieved only if the child is exposed to the art at an early age and ideally from within his own family.

CHAPTER 5

Stylized Acting

THE WORD Kabuki is used to describe a variety of different types of theater and dance, with varying degrees of stylization depending on the play. Generally the *jidaimono* plays set in Japan's historical or legendary past tend to contain a greater degree of stylization than other plays. There are certain stylized conventions in movement, music, and speech that are part of the actor's technique and which, although quite simple, do need to be explained to people seeing Kabuki for the first time.

Mie (dramatic poses)

The dramatic poses called *mie* are the high points of Kabuki performance. There are many kinds of *mie*, and depending on the type of play they may be highly stylized as seen in *jidaimono*, or somewhat more natural, better suited to the *sewamono* plays of the common people.

Mie generally follow a pattern, serving to focus our attention on a particular character or characters at an important moment during the play. *Mie* crystallize the action into a formal picture. More than mere focal points, *mie* are used to express to the audience a climax of great emotional tension.

To perform a *mie* the actor must physically and emotionally wind himself up to the desired emotion, be it anger, fear, indignation, or surprise. Most *mie* are accompanied only by the beating of the wooden clappers *(tsuke),* visible to the right, under the proscenium arch. They are struck in a pattern called *ba-tan,* the two beats of which serve as a framework for the climax of the *mie,* in which the actor, while holding the pose rotates his head toward his adversary and crosses one eye, the other looking straight ahead. The pose is then dissolved, the music begins again, and the play continues. Certain *mie* in classical plays are named after the attitude in which they are performed. The *ishinage no mie,* in which one arm is raised as if throwing a stone; the *hashiramaki no mie*, with one arm and one leg wrapped around a pillar; and the *genroku mie* (Fig. 20) (named for the Genroku period of Japanese history, 1688–1704) are famous examples. Female characters in Kabuki do not perform *mie* but may assume a similar pose, without the crossed eyes, known as *kimari.* The rotation of the head is also softer, more feminine, and less vigorous, a good example being the final pose of Hanako as, assuming the form of a serpent, she mounts the bell at the end of the dance *Musume Dojoji.*

In *Kanjincho* there are six major *mie* which connect the action of the play. The first is performed as Benkei hides the scroll from Togashi and expresses the tension at this crucial moment. The second comes at the end of the scroll-reading when, in keeping with the religious tone of the scroll, Benkei performs the *mie* in the attitude of the god Fudo Myoo. Next comes the *genroku mie* at the end of the confrontation with Togashi, and during his tale of their battles, Benkei performs the *ishinage no mie.* The final two *mie* come at the end of the play. Benkei and Togashi pose together as the curtain closes, expressing the tension between them. Benkei performs the last *mie* as he winds up for his famous bounding exit.

Ki and Tsuke (wooden clappers)

The most distinctive sound in the Kabuki theater is first heard about five minutes before the play begins. A sharp wooden "clack" comes from the backstage area and gradually becomes louder and nearer to the stage. As the curtain is run open, the beats become quicker and quicker as the scene is revealed. There is a pause, and one final "clack," or *chon* as it is called in Japanese, signals the beginning of the play. This is the sound of the signal clappers called *ki* or *hyoshigi* (two rectangular blocks of oak about twenty-five centimeters long and seven centimeters square). They are carved in a slightly curved shape so that when they are struck together they come in contact only at one point and so produce a finer tone.

Ki are used first to signal the actors backstage that the performance is about to begin and again to signal the beginning and ending of the play. The final *chon* is the signal for the *kakegoe* callers on the third floor of the theater to begin their closing shouts of appreciation.

Unlike the man who beats the *ki,* the *tsuke* beater, in the right-hand corner under the proscenium arch, is in full view of the audience. Kneeling on a small cushion, he beats two blocks on a wooden board laid on the stage. Though these blocks are also called *ki* or *hyoshigi,* they are squarer and more solid than the others, and produce heavier sounds. These sounds are called *tsuke* and are used for various imitations throughout the play. During a stylized fight scene, or *tachimawari,* there is no actual sword contact, so the sound of clashing weapons is added by the *tsuke* beater who carefully times his blows with the actors' movements. The sound of running feet is also made by the *tsuke* in a pattern called *bata-bata.*

Most importantly, *tsuke* are used to accompany *mie* poses, usually with a simple two-beat pattern called *ba-tan*. The first beat, the *ba*, is hit as the actor strikes the pose. Then, as he rotates his head and glares, the *mie* is completed by the second, *tan* beat. The *tsuke* beater, or *tsuke uchi* as he is called, has the great responsibility of not only timing his beats to the actor's movements but also feeling the emotional climax of the *mie* with the actor.

The most exciting pattern of all uses both *ki* and *tsuke* as the grand climax to a play. The *tsuke* beats begin loud and slow and accelerate at a furious pace. Suddenly they soften, quickly return to maximum volume, slow down again, and stop. The characters assume their final tableau and a sharp *chon* of the *ki* signals the end of the play. A final grand *mie* accompanied by *ba-tan* is heard, and the *ki* accelerate again as the curtain closes.

Roppo (stylized exits)

At the end of the play *Kanjincho*, the hero Benkei poses alone on the *hanamichi*. Although this is a moment of repose, the audience is tense in anticipation of Benkei's joyful bounding exit along the *hanamichi*. This exit is known as the *tobi roppo*, or "flying exit." Benkei twirls his staff dramatically into position under his arm and strikes a final grand *mie* pose. Then to great applause and shouts from the callers among the audience, he bounds off down the *hanamichi*, hopping on one leg then the other. He gains such momentum that out of sight of the audience, in the small greenroom at the end of the *hanamichi*, one of his assistants will catch him to prevent his crashing into the wall.

Although *roppo* are usually seen as stylized exits, they may in fact be performed as part of an entrance or even during the play itself. In *Hiragana Seisuiki*, Matsuemon performs a *roppo* from the *hanamichi* to the great pine tree that is in the center of the main stage.

The origin of the word *roppo*, which is made up of the

characters for "six" and "direction," is unclear but may refer to the six directions—heavenward, earthward, north, south, east, and west—in which the arms and legs are supposed to move. Another possibility is that *roppo* is an adaptation of *tanzen*, an affected gait adopted by the dandies of Edo when walking from the public baths. Actors soon began to emulate this walk, and new, more intricate variations were added. Posing with the arms slightly outstretched on either side of the body, the actor moves his right arm and right leg forward together; the left foot moves along to join the right, and then the same movement is repeated with the left arm and leg. Sukeroku, at the end of his opening dance of entry, performs a *tanzen roppo* as he struts onto the main stage to greet the awaiting courtesans.

Today only a few *roppo* styles survive. Although each had its own characteristics they usually involved, to some degree, hopping alternately on one leg and then the other.

The *kitsune roppo*, or "fox exit," takes its name from the animal-like leaps and bounds performed by the actor while holding his hands up to his chest with the fingers tucked in like paws. It is most frequently seen at the end of Act VI, the *michiyuki* or "travel dance," in *Yoshitsune Senbon Zakura* (Fig. 11).

The *kumo-te tako-ashi roppo* (literally "spider hands and octopus legs exit") is performed by the villain Tonbe (Fig. 33) in the play *Shinrei Yaguchi no Watashi*. The name of the *roppo* comes from Tonbe's movements as he, an old ferryman with white beard and hair, staggers along the *hanamichi* in pursuit of his enemy.

The *keisei roppo* (courtesan exit) is perhaps the most bizarre *roppo* of all and is performed by the courtesan at the end of *Miyajima no Danmari*. The actor first hops along on the tall clogs worn by courtesans and then adopts a posturing gait in which he parades slowly with each foot tracing a figure eight in the air before lowering to the ground.

Although *roppo* usually have little relevance to the actual drama, they are enjoyed as a tour de force, much like a particularly difficult and exciting octave passage in a piano concerto.

Tachimawari (fight scenes)

As reflected in Kabuki, premodern Japan was a violent society in which a strict code of behavior was enforced both from orders by the Shogunate and by the samurai's Bushido philosophy. However, violence in Kabuki takes a back seat to the art's aesthetics, and in general, effects such as stage blood are used infrequently and with restraint. The horror of suicide scenes, for example, is suggested by the power of the acting rather than realistic displays of gore. This also holds true for Kabuki fight scenes, and *tachimawari,* as they are called, take on an ethereal, mimelike quality that belies any suggestion of actual inflicted violence.

Tachimawari vary in length from short skirmishes to spectacularly staged sections lasting ten or fifteen minutes. The fight scenes are accompanied by background music called *geza,* which may be expectedly lively or rather slow and languorous, adding to the mood of ethereal unreality. There is no actual physical contact, and the blows of the hand or sword are mimed and suggested by the rhythmic sounds of the wooden *tsuke* clappers.

In a standard *tachimawari* the hero is attacked by about twenty men who have come not to kill but to arrest him. He fends them off effortlessly, moving from one pose to the next, climaxing each tableau with a *mie* pose. Whether the hero uses a sword or just his bare hands, the attackers seem powerless against him. Shouting *Nao!* they attack him one by one, but with a mere flick of his hands he sends them flying through the air or into a somersault called a *tonbo,* which signifies a kill. After the *tonbo,* the conventions of the kill being satisfied, the fallen actor gets up, runs to the rear of the set and prepares to join in again. The adversaries may also be armed, but it is more usual for them to brandish objects such as buckets and skillfully incorporate them into a picturesque tableau. Occasionally a group may attack the hero with small branches of cherry blossom. These men are called *hana-yoten* (literally, "flower pattern") for the costumes they wear, and may be seen most frequently in the travel dance of Kanpei and Okaru from *Chushingura*. The blossoms, while satisfying the idea of a weapon, also serve to enhance the picturesque scene.

Tachimawari are choreographed by a specialist in the art known as *tateshi*. He works out the tableau and the various connecting movements in small line-drawings and then coaches the actors during rehearsals. *Tachimawari* is one of the few areas of Kabuki subject to change, and a freshly choreographed fight is prepared for each run of the play. There are many standard movements which are chosen and combined to form the complete *tachimawari*. Some of these movements are *chidori*, which shows the hero parrying the blows of the mob as they pass alternately by him to the left and right; *ebizori*, an exaggerated movement demonstrating the great strength of the hero, in which he stamps forward and the whole row of men fall over backward; and *yamagata* (mountain shape), in which swords are swung to the right and left of the opponent and create the shape of a mountain.

It is most common for the fight to end with the hero routing the men and sending them fleeing down the *hanamichi*. The hero then strikes a pose on the *hanamichi* and the play continues. The picturesque tableaux, dramatic poses, thrilling acrobatics, and overall surrealism of *tachimawari* include the most entertaining and thrilling of Kabuki elements.

Serifu (speech)

Speech in Kabuki, known as *serifu*, is stylized to a greater or lesser degree depending on the type of play. *Sewamono* usually employ a style of speaking very similar to modern Japanese.

Although some of the modes of speech are now considered old-fashioned, in general the style is rather natural and readily understood. Speeches in *jidaimono,* on the other hand, are more likely to be delivered rhythmically to musical accompaniment and occasionally are so formal that even Japanese, if they are not familiar with the idiom, have some difficulty understanding them.

In Japanese literature, great importance is placed on word rhythm. The very nature of the language, in which vowels almost always follow consonants, makes it very susceptible to a sing-song style of delivery. This may be further emphasized by the groupings of syllables used in the composition of Japanese poetry. The best known of these is the seven-five grouping, *shichi-go-cho,* which is employed in the writing of haiku poems. The following example shows the syllable splits to make clear the rhythm:

> *Yo-za-ku-ra-ya* (5)
> *Ma-ta-Su-ke-ro-ku-no* (7)
> *Ke-n-ka-za-ta* (5)

> Evening cherry blossoms,
> And once more
> Sukeroku quarrels.

Speeches spoken in rhythm, similar to this haiku about the hero of the play *Sukeroku,* abound in Kabuki, and are usually accompanied by the shamisen. Often delivered at highly emotional moments in the drama, this style of speech is called *ito ni noru,* or "riding the strings." The actor is said to ride on the strings of the shamisen, meaning that his speech and sometimes his gestures are timed to the rhythm of the shamisen accompaniment.

Rhythm is also important in the two types of shared dialogue, "divided speech," *wari-zerifu*, and "passed-along speech," *watari-zerifu*. In *wari-zerifu* two characters divide up a long speech, alternating the lines between them. Similarly, *watari-zerifu* is divided, but by more characters, and is often spoken by a line of ladies-in-waiting or by feudal lords, who set the scene before the main characters enter. Dialogue is passed along from one to the other, building up to a climax in which they all share the final line. Speeches by such minor characters often serve as a prelude and are not usually important to the drama. However, the musical flow of *wari-* and *watari-zerifu* is very enjoyable and is one of Kabuki's most characteristic features.

An argument is often brought to a climax by the technique known as *kuriage*. Actors alternately say *Saa! Saa! Saa!* (Well! Well! Well!), with increasing speed and intensity until one of the characters emerges dominant and continues the speech.

Pitch is also important in the delivery of Kabuki speeches, and each type has a prescribed vocal range. The most discernible is that of the *onnagata* roles, which are all spoken in a falsetto. Although all actors are capable of producing a woman's voice, *onnagata* specialists use a falsetto nearly all the time and may achieve a remarkably convincing delivery. While a frequent Kabuki-goer may come to accept *onnagata* voices as natural, they always have a certain stylized hard edge and are never realistic.

In male roles, differences in pitch depend on the character's age and social status. Young men, and in particular young aristocrats, speak in a relatively high pitch, similar to an *onnagata*. In fact, roles such as Yoshitsune in *Kanjincho* are often taken by *onnagata* actors. Older men, and especially characters of an evil disposition, adopt an excessively gruff, deep, masculine voice.

Two types of speech that may occasionally be heard are *akutai*, a speech of abuse, and *tsurane*, a speech in which a character (and sometimes the actor too) identifies himself to the audience.

The most famous example of an *akutai* occurs in *Sukeroku*, in which Sukeroku's lover, the courtesan Agemaki, abuses the evil Ikyu, who lusts after her. Not only the words but the delivery as well are of vital importance. Certain words and syllables are drawn out, almost sung, and at the end, amused by her own wit, Agemaki bursts into malicious laughter:

> *Moshi, Ikyu-san, Omae to Sukeroku-san, ko narabete miru toki wa, kochira wa rippa na otoko buri, kochira wa ijinowaru so na. Tatoete iwaba, yuki to sumi. Suzuri no umi mo, Naruto no umi mo, umi to iu ji wa hitotsu demo. Fukai to asai wa kyaku to mabu. Mabu ga nakereba joro wa yami. Kuragari de mitemo, Omae to Sukeroku-san tori chigaete yoi mono kai na! Ho! Ho! Ho! Ho!*

"Ikyu! If I compare you to Sukeroku, here [holding up her long silver pipe] is a real man, and here [extending one finger] an evil old rake. The two of you are as different as snow and ink, like the water in an inkstone and the sea at Naruto. Deep and shallow like a lover and a mere customer. Without a lover a prostitute's life is black. But even in the dark it would be a fine thing if I mistook you for Sukeroku! Ho! Ho! Ho! Ho!"

In *tsurane*, a character identifies himself for the benefit of both the other characters on stage and those in the audience. The most famous example of this occurs in *Shibaraku*. The hero, Kamakura Gongoro, enters along the *hanamichi* and stops to deliver a long speech in which he not only announces his name but also, in extremely formal language, works in references to the Ichikawa line of actors. This is done because *Shibaraku* is one of the Juhachiban collection, the property of the Ichikawa family. He mentions the family crest of the three square rice measures, the persimmon color of his costume (the Ichikawa color), the peony secondary crest, and the bombastic *aragoto* style in which he is acting.

Kata (form or model)

At first sight Kabuki appears to be a static art whose every aspect—costume, set, movement, or vocal delivery—is rigidly fixed by tradition, with no opportunity for a director to influence or interpret the play. The leading actor takes the director's role, ensuring that all his fellow actors perform in the manner prescribed by their forebears. Within this rigidity, however, there do exist many small variations, determined and brought into play by the actor playing the role according to his family's tradition. These subtle variations, known as the *kata* of a particular actor or acting line, will become apparent after one has seen the play performed many times by different actors.

Kata actually means "form or model," but here it refers to differences in costume or makeup and, in particular, variations in the performance of important moments in the play. Variations may at times be quite obvious and at others so tiny that the average viewer will be unaware of them. During the eighteenth and nineteenth centuries, when Kabuki was still developing, various actors sought to mold and influence the drama. By the Meiji era, however, most *kata* had become fixed and would be handed down to the next generation. *Kata* are performed as treasured and respected possessions and may be changed or tampered with only in exceptional circumstances.

Some of the simplest *kata* are related to costume. Matsuomaru, the leading character of the play *Terakoya* (The Village School), usually wears a magnificent outer robe decorated with a snow-covered pine tree on a black background. However, the Otowa-ya *kata* for this costume stipulates that the background be gray. Otowa-ya is the acting-house name, the *yago,* of the Onoe Kikugoro line of actors. In recent times, this costume would be adopted by the late Nakamura Kanzaburo XVII, the son-in-law of Kikugoro VI (1885–1949), and by Kikugoro VII were he to perform this role. Similarly, the color of the scroll read by Benkei during one of the dramatic climaxes of *Kanjincho* differs according to the actor. Sometimes the back of the scroll is plain black, sometimes patterned, sometimes speckled gray.

In the same play Benkei dances the final celebrated "dance of longevity," the *ennen no mai,* entirely on the main stage. The actor Matsumoto Koshiro IX, however, performs this section with an old *kata,* whereby he dances onto the *hanamichi* at one point. At present, Koshiro is one of the few actors who do this. Another famous *kata* from the same play comes at Yoshitsune's entrance at the beginning of the play. Yoshitsune enters along the *hanamichi* and, turning back, gazes up at the surrounding mountains. As Nakamura Utaemon V (1866–1940) grew older, he was unable to lean back and perform this section. He therefore invented a *kata* by which he could execute the movement without twisting his body, a *kata* which now even agile actors perform.

At one point during *Sukeroku* the evil Ikyu threatens to crush Sukeroku like an irritating mosquito. Having said these lines most actors stamp forward with their right foot, mime-crushing an insect between their palms, and glare. Matsumoto Koshiro IX, however, performs an almost certainly older and more dramatic *kata,* by which he executes a full-blown *mie* pose complete with accompanying *tsuke* beats. Although only a minor addition, this *mie* conveys strength and the idea that Ikyu is an adversary to be dealt with, not just a doddery old man. This is particularly important since the role of Ikyu is, in fact, often played by an elderly actor.

Some *kata* may seem trivial, but they are still performed and greatly enjoyed because of their historic association. For example, the character Naozamurai, from the play of the same name, enters a *soba* (noodle) shop and orders *soba* and saké. Ichimura Uzaemon XV invented a realistic *kata* for this scene in which Naozamurai notices a speck of dust in his saké and flicks it out with a chopstick. This movement takes a mere two or three seconds yet is a detail of great interest to viewers who know their history. The more knowledgeable *kakegoe* callers may even shout out to the actor *"Komakai!"* (What detail!) in appreciation.

Dances often vary widely due to various *kata*. Actors may perform totally different versions of what is supposed to be the same dance. In the older version of the dance *Sagi Musume* (The Heron Maiden), for example, the maiden ends the dance by posing on a red dais. This Kabukiesque approach was completely changed by Onoe Kikugoro VI, who, inspired by Anna Pavlova's "Dying Swan," has the heron collapse to the ground and expire at the end of the dance.

Kata are still learned by rote, by observing and imitating a father, uncle, older brother or senior actor, or by oral instruction. Increasingly, however, actors are beginning to study the methods of past actors. As in other Japanese arts, students are not expected to understand or even question the reasoning behind a particular *kata*. Appreciation of a *kata* and its perfect execution is expected to come only after many years of constant performance and repetition. This may, albeit rarely, lead an actor to make changes of his own and give birth to a completely new *kata*.

CHAPTER **6**

Music

THE FIRST character of the word Kabuki, *ka*, means "song" and implies all music. In Kabuki— the characters for which are literally translated "song and dance art"—music is of vital importance. Only the most modern plays attempt to do without it. A full discussion of Kabuki's music, however, does not lie within the scope of this book. It is extremely difficult to describe an aural art in print, and even with the inclusion of printed musical examples, an understanding of the music is really possible only with an accompanying recording. Readers with a particular interest in this area are referred to the most thorough work on the subject in English, *Japanese Music and Musical Instruments*, by William P. Malm. Commercially produced recordings of Kabuki and other forms of Japanese traditional music are also available.

Music is heard almost continually throughout most Kabuki plays. Sometimes two or three different styles of music, played from different parts of the stage, will sound at various points during the play or even simultaneously. Musicians usually play either behind the grille incorporated into the set on the left of the stage, or appear in formal costume, on stage with the actors. The various groups may alternate throughout the play, or one group may play for one section only.

Geza (background music)

Background music is known as *geza*, which is also the term for the small room seen through the grille on the left of the stage. From the semidarkness of this room the musicians look out through the grille to the stage or *hanamichi*, and, timing their music to the play and the actors' movements, add background music, atmosphere, and sound effects to the unfolding scene.

Apart from the singers, the instrument central to *geza* is the three-stringed shamisen. This lutelike instrument, played with a heavy plectrum, was introduced from China around the year 1560, and its popularity grew together with the development of Kabuki. Shamisen are made in various sizes. The largest, which has the biggest tone, is used to accompany *gidayu* chanting. The shamisen strings are tuned in three different ways: *honchoshi, niagari,* and *sansagari.* There is no fixed pitch, but the intervals remain the same and are (in ascending order), approximately, B below middle C, E, B for *honchoshi;* B, F, B sharp for the *niagari;* and B, E, A for the *sansagari.*

The other principal instruments of *geza* are the Noh flute *(nohkan);* the bamboo flute *(take-bue);* the shoulder-drums *(ko-tsuzumi),* which are struck with one to four fingers; the side-drums *(o-tsuzumi),* which are held on the hip and also struck with thimbled fingers to give a drier, sharper tone; the stick-drum *(taiko);* the very large drum *(o-daiko);* and various other percussion instruments such as gongs, wood blocks, and bells of varying timbres.

For plays with no on-stage musical accompaniment, background music is played almost continually to add atmosphere and mood. For the famous opening of Act VII of *Chushingura,* set in the Ichiriki teahouse in the Gion pleasure quarter in Kyoto, the lively song immediately sets the scene and evokes the gay mood of the pleasure quarters. The rapid shamisen music at the beginning of the "Mustering Scene" in *Benten Kozo*, before the five thieves enter holding umbrellas, imitates the falling rain on the banks of the Inase River in Kamakura.

Apart from songs and pieces, *geza* also includes more obvious sound effects, although these tend to be highly stylized. Falling snow makes virtually no sound at all, but the slow throbbing of the *o-daiko* suggests the muffled world of a snow-covered landscape. For the beginning of *Shunkan*, the waves lapping Devil's Island are suggested by undulating drumbeats called *nami no oto*, or "wave sounds." Many such musical sound-effect patterns are used to imitate wind, rain, or running water, and often a drum pattern, for example, will accompany a song or shamisen piece to further add atmosphere.

The recognition and appreciation of *geza* pieces and sound effects depend largely on familiarity with the idiom. Despite the large number of such motifs, they are easily recognizable and consistent from play to play. Supernatural happenings, for example, are inevitably accompanied by the drum pattern described by the onomatopoeic word *doro-doro*. Such patterns aid the theatergoer in an understanding and appreciation of the unfolding drama.

Gidayu (chanting)

Although plays derived from the puppet theater often employ *geza*, they principally incorporate chanting with shamisen accompaniment, a style known as *gidayu*. *Gidayu* constitutes the basic narration for Bunraku puppet plays. This form of chanted narration, originated by Takemoto Gidayu (1651–1714), is extremely strenuous, and actors study it from an early age to develop their voices. In Bunraku, the chanter uses a variety of vocal timbres to speak for the puppets. The chanting is highly dramatic, and the chanter is almost as much an actor as a musician. In Kabuki, on the other hand, this role is predominantly confined to providing comments on the characters' thoughts and emotions and to describing the on-stage scene. The shamisen used is larger than the standard instrument and of a more sonorous timbre. The calls made by the shamisen player are also very important, serving as timing signals to the chanter and actors, and as up-beats such as when a jazz musician counts in a piece with ". . .three, four." The chanter and shamisen may be concealed behind a bamboo screen on the raised floor to the right of the stage, but for the most part they appear *degatari,* in full view of the audience, on a revolving platform under this screen.

Nagauta

The *geza* musicians and singers actually play in a style known as *nagauta,* or "long song." Alternately lively and rhythmic and melodic and plaintive, *nagauta* came to fruition in Edo between 1716 and 1736 and is the oldest form of what we may call pure Kabuki music, evolving together with the theater. As its name implies, *nagauta* was designed as an extended style of melodic music, suitable for the accompaniment of lengthy dances. The words do not necessarily tell a story and, in fact, may often be a mere melodic recitation of names of famous mountains or places. This style is also employed for many of Kabuki's most famous dances and dance-dramas when the musicians appear *debayashi,* on raised, red felt-covered platforms along the rear of the set. Approximately eight singers and eight shamisen players kneel on the upper platform, with the ranking musicians in the middle. Along the bottom row sit or kneel the *taiko* stick drummer, *otsuzumi* side drummer, two or three *ko-tsuzumi* shoulder drummers, and the flute player, who plays both the *nohkan* and *take-bue* flutes. *Nagauta* became so popular that it is now the most common style in Kabuki and is used in many great plays and dances such as *Kanjincho*, *Tsuchigumo* (The Earth Spider), the lion dances, *Kagami Jishi* and *Ren Jishi*, and *Musume Dojoji*, the most famous dance in the repertoire.

Kiyomoto, Tokiwazu, and Kato Bushi

Three additional styles, *kiyomoto*, *tokiwazu*, and *kato bushi*, also deserve brief mention. *Kato bushi*, an amateur style, is actually heard in only one play, *Sukeroku*, in which it comes at the beginning, and for the famous *deha*, the dance of entry on the *hanamichi*. *Kato bushi* musicians may pay enormous sums of money for the privilege of taking part in the performance of *Sukeroku*.

The intense style, *kiyomoto* was originated by Kiyomoto Enjudayu (1777–1825) around 1814 and is characterized by very high, falsetto vocal lines. *Kiyomoto* is often heared as an accompaniment to love scenes. At present, the greatest exponent of *kiyomoto* is Kiyomoto Shizutayu, who is now about ninety years old. Western singers usually stop performing during their fifties, but in Japanese music, where the whole concept of a beautiful voice and good vocal tone is different, it is common for singers to remain active to an advanced age. What in the West is called "purity" of tone is less important in Japanese singing, and the gruffness that comes with age is not considered to detract from the enjoyment of the vocal line.

Tokiwazu, originated by Tokiwazu Mojidayu (1709–81) is less often heard in the theater. It is similar to *kiyomoto* in that a high falsetto is employed, but the vocal lines are usually less dramatically intense. One dance-drama, *Momijigari* (The Maple Viewing), is an excellent vehicle for comparing the various styles of Kabuki music. Not only *geza* but *nagauta*, *kiyomoto*, *tokiwazu*, and *gidayu* are heard at various points in the play.

The Kabuki viewer should notice two other small points with regard to the musicians. First, etiquette calls for the *nagauta*, *kiyomoto*, and *tokiwazu* singers to pick up their closed fans while singing and to lay them down again at the end of a section. Second, the musicians can be identified immediately by the stands that hold copies of the text. (All the music, either played or sung, is performed from memory.) The grandest one is the tasseled, heavy black stand of the *gidayu* chanter. *Nagauta* uses a very simple, flat-topped stand formed by crossed pieces of lightly colored wood. The *kiyomoto* stand is plain black with a square base, and the *tokiwazu* stand is an elegant, red stand on tall curved legs.

CHAPTER *7*

Costumes, Wigs, and Makeup

 AS FOR MANY other aspects of Kabuki, it is usually tradition that determines the costume for a particular role. Although Kabuki costumes, called *isho*, are justly famous for their color and beauty, the costumes that are worn for *sewamono* are very close to the practical, everyday wear of the lower and middle classes in the Edo period. This clothing is similar to the traditional dress worn today, and although elegant, is often drabber than what many people expect from Kabuki.

The standard dress for both male and female characters is the kimono, which in Japanese means simply a "thing to wear." Male and female kimono do differ in some respects, but the basic form is the same, a long-sleeved garment tied around the waist with a sash, or obi. The kimono may be ankle length or, for female characters, it may trail on the ground behind the wearer. For women, the back of the collar is usually low, exposing the nape of the neck, which is considered an erotic part of the body. Sleeve length also varies with the role, the longer sleeves being worn by young girls.

The standard kimono for the wife of a samurai is called a *kokumochi,* as worn by Tonami, Genzo's wife in *Terakoya* (The Village School). A *koku* is a measure of rice, a unit used to express the salary of a samurai. *Kokumochi* means simply "rice-payment holder" and thus is an indication of social status. This kimono is usually a plain dark maroon with a black obi and collar. The only ornamentation is the character's family crest sewn onto the breast, sleeves, and back of the kimono.

The formal dress of the samurai is the *kamishimo,* the costume worn not only by the actors but also by all the musicians on stage. The *kamishimo* consists of a plain kimono, over which are worn wide trousers called *hakama,* and the wide, stiffened shoulder wings known as the *kataginu.* In historical scenes set within the confines of a palace, the long trailing *naga-bakama* (*naga,* long; *bakama,* trousers) may be worn. These are kicked out behind before moving off as in Act III of *Chushingura.* Morano deliberately insults Enya Hangan by kicking his *naga-bakama* into Hangan's face as he turns away from him.

Naga-bakama are also worn by envoy characters such as the evil Seno in the play *Shunkan.* The trailing trousers are here tucked up to leave the legs free for easy movement. Under the *hakama* the actor may wear tights and mysterious little pads tied just under his knees. These are called *sanri-ate* and are meant to cover the points used for moxa, a folk-medicine treatment in which dried herbs are burned on the skin as a cautery.

Katsura (wigs)

A Kabuki actor never appears on stage without a wig. The wigs are created individually for each actor by making a copper mold of the head. The wigmaker covers this with a silk cloth onto which individual strands of real hair are sewn. Then a wig artist called a *toko-yama* dresses the wig in the correct style. The four or five *toko-yama* who work in the Kabuki-za are each responsible for several wigs which they carefully dress and take to the actor's dressing room in time for the performance. When the actor comes off stage the first thing to be removed is his wig, which is returned to the *toko-yama* to be redressed for the next performance.

After women were banned from the stage in 1629, the youths who continued Kabuki ceased to shave their forelocks, as was the custom for men at that time. An edict forbidding this practice was issued by the government, and these actors took to covering the shaven patch with a purple cloth known as a *katsura*. In time, the word *katsura* came to mean an entire wig of hair. Even today the wigs of certain female roles still have this small purple patch (or gray in the case of an old woman) known as the *murasaki boshi* attached at the front. Though now only a decoration, it reminds us of Kabuki's origins.

Hundreds of subtle variations exist in wig styles, all of which give clues to the character's social standing, age, temperament, and even occupation. The normal shaven crown of the male wig may have a growth of hair which usually indicates a samurai who has fallen on hard times and has too many cares to bother about going to the barber. In one particular variation, known as the *gojunichi*, or "fifty-day" wig, as worn by Matsuomaru (Fig. 27) in the play *Terakoya*, long hair indicates that the character has not been able to visit the barber for some time due to illness. The *chasen*, or "tea whisk" wig, with a backward-hanging topknot and possibly hair at the front, indicates a youth who will have the crown of his head shaven on attaining manhood.

Female wigs also indicate social status and are divided into five main types: those for courtesans, geisha, princesses or girls of high birth, girls of the lower classes, and married women of the middle classes. In earlier times Japanese women wore their long hair loose down their backs, but with the introduction of an oil-based dressing that held the hair in place, a complicated system of knots and twists became fashionable. The pins and ornaments used to hold the hair also became an important part of the style. Chidori, the diving girl in *Shunkan,* has her hair dressed in the ponytail *(uma no shippo)* style, while the intricate twist *(katahazushi)* at the rear of Masaoka's wig in *Meiboku Sendai Hagi* (Fig. 13) befits an upper-class, mature woman in the service of the aristocracy. The most gorgeous of the female wigs is the heavily ornamented *hyogo,* worn by courtesans of the highest rank, such as Agemaki in *Sukeroku.*

There are certain trick wigs in which fasteners may be pulled out so the piled-up hair cascades down around the shoulders. This technique is employed in death scenes such as that of Kanpei in Act VI of *Chushingura* and in the ghost play *Yotsuya Kaidan.* Oiwa wears a special wig that sheds its hair as she combs it—a result of poison administered by the evil husband.

Kesho and Kumadori (makeup)

Kabuki makeup *(kesho)* may be separated into two distinct types: the standard makeup employed for the majority of characters, and *kumadori,* used for superheroes and villains and seen most frequently in the *aragoto* acting style.

Realistic facial tones are usually seen in the portrayal of the lower classes, while the majority of Kabuki upper-class characters use pure white as their makeup base. In Japan white skin has traditionally been associated with the aristocracy, the logical reasoning behind this being that they were not exposed to the sun while working in the fields. However, in certain plays, such as *Benten Kozo* or *Kirare Yosa,* in which low-class characters play the major role, a pure white base is employed. As principal characters they were required to artistically project to the audience, and in the days before electric lighting, the white base helped to accomplish this.

Except in the case of young children, actors always put on their own makeup and begin their preparation by tying a cloth known as a *habutae* around the upper forehead and over the hair. This holds the hair in place, protects it, and provides a flat surface on which to put the wig. The face and neck are first covered with oil and then with a thick covering of white cream known as *oshiroi*. When a female role is being played, the *oshiroi* will also extend a long way down the back because of the very low back-collar line of the kimono. The *habutae* where it is over the forehead is also covered with makeup, extending high enough to be covered by the crown of the wig. A touch of pink powder may be applied to give a blush to the cheeks.

The white base obliterates the actor's features, in particular the lips and eyebrows. Eyebrows are painted on somewhat higher than actual eyebrows, and the eyes are subtly lined in black for men and red for women. Lip rouge and black are used to produce a downward curve to the mouths of the men. The female mouth is also red and made smaller, with a slightly thicker lower lip—the ideal of feminine beauty. There are many eyeline, eyebrow, and lip styles, which have been stylized and conventionalized to suggest character and social status. It was also the custom in premodern Japan for married women to shave their eyebrows and blacken their teeth with *ohaguro*, a substance made from black sugar and resin.

It was Ichikawa Danjuro I who introduced the *aragoto* style of acting, characterized by exaggerated costumes, movements, and vocal delivery. To complement those features and further enhance his fierce and forbidding demeanor, Danjuro painted his face with broad red and black stripes, a style called *kumadori*.

The origins of Danjuro's *kumadori* remain unclear, though the bloom of the peony and the painted faces of Chinese opera are often cited as sources of inspiration. Chinese opera's identification of role-types by the makeup is indeed similar to Kabuki's, but it remains doubtful how much of an inspiration this could have been for Danjuro and his successors, none of whom were likely to have seen Chinese opera. Furthermore, Chinese opera makeup and *kumadori* differ greatly in one all-important respect. Whereas the Chinese style calls for the face to be covered in a highly colored abstract pattern, *kumadori* is more subtle and is

15. Bando Yasosuke V applies *kumadori* makeup for the role of Tadanobu from Act II of *Yoshitsune Senbon Zakura*.

based on lines drawn deliberately to enhance the facial muscles and bone structure. Such lines greatly increase the face's expressiveness. It is thought that the lines of paint could represent veins, the red color used by heroic characters representing a flush of righteous indignation, and the villain's blue shade indicating his cold-blooded nature. *Kumadori* may also be seen on arms and legs, not as makeup but as patterns painted on tights and long sleeves.

As Kabuki developed as an art, so too did *kumadori*. At one time there may have been over one hundred different types in use. Today there are far fewer, with only ten or fifteen being commonly seen. Styles range from the subtle lip rouge and eye highlights of the *mukimi-guma* style for the famous role of Sukeroku, to the more complex *nihon suji-guma* for Gongoro, the hero of *Shibaraku*. There are also special designs such as the one created to portray the earth spider in *Tsuchigumo*.

After the lines are painted on with a brush or the fingertip, the hard lines are smudged with the finger to soften and blend them into the white base. Although the pattern for a certain role is rigidly fixed by tradition, subtle differences inevitably occur in the breadth and intensity of the lines, dictated in part by the actor's physical features. Despite the confines of tradition, the way in which an actor applies his *kumadori* is as personal as a signature (Fig. 15).

Oshiguma (face pressings)

The curtain closes to shouts and applause, and assistants hasten to remove the actor's heavy costume and wig. The actor then hurries to his dressing room where he takes an oblong towel of silk, closes his eyes, and with great care presses the material first to his forehead. Then, working his way slowly down his face, he presses it around his eyes, under his nose, round to his ears, and beneath his chin. The material covers his face like a shroud. As the streaks of makeup begin to show through the perspiration-dampened cloth, an assistant presses the actor's fingers to the parts he has missed or that do not show up clearly. Then he peels off the silk to reveal the *oshiguma*, a perfect mirror-image of the actor's face in that particular role on that particular day. This procedure is likely to be repeated every day of the month-long run, and when the pressings are completely dry, the actor signs, dates, and stamps them with his personal seal. *Oshiguma* are highly valued mementos of the actor's performance and may be given away to fans or occasionally sold for a charitable cause.

Despite the great age of the *kumadori* makeup style, the practice of taking an *oshiguma* appears to be a comparatively recent phenomenon, initiated by Ichikawa Danjuro IX (1838–1903) in the Meiji era. He is said to have hit upon the idea while pressing a cloth to his face to remove the makeup for the main

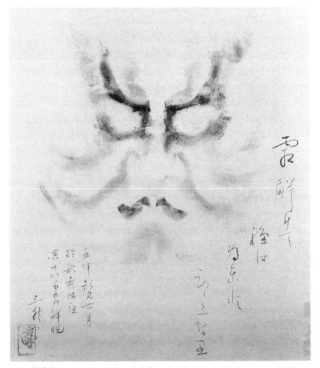

16. *Oshiguma* taken by Ichikawa Sansho V (Danjuro X) in 1932. The role is Kagekiyo from *Gedatsu*. Makeup on silk. From the collection of the author.

role of *Shibaraku*. Advances in the quality of the actual makeup, which enabled it to stick and remain on the cloth, may have also contributed to the discovery. In any case the practice soon became common among star actors.

The subtle differences in the way each actor applies his makeup may be clearly seen when comparing *oshiguma* of actors in the same role.

There should never be more pressings than the actual number

of performances in a Kabuki run, usually about twenty-five. Veteran actor Ichimura Uzaemon XVII warns against the practice of repainting the face solely for the purpose of taking an *oshiguma*. Should this be done, he says, the *oshiguma* is *iki ga nai* (devoid of life). Indeed, it is the life behind the sightless eyes of the *oshiguma* that crosses the bridge of time separating us from the actor and his performance (Fig. 16).

CHAPTER **8**

Sets and Props

SETS, PROPS, staging devices, and curtains are essential elements of Kabuki. The sets themselves are referred to as *o-dogu*, a category that takes in special effects such as the devices that enable characters to fly across the stage or appear suddenly from beneath it. The props are divided generally into *ko-dogu*, or hand props such as fans, and *de-dogu*, small objects such as lanterns and braziers that appear in domestic scenes.

O-dogu (sets)

Kabuki stage sets, known as *o-dogu*, are really quite simple in design but may be lavishly painted and extremely colorful. They are constructed both on and behind the stage, and the occasional sound of hammering during the performance does not appear to disturb the Japanese audience. The entire stage may be presented as the interior of one room, or the front and side of a house may be shown against a painted landscape. In this case the house is usually built on a raised platform with three steps called the *sandan* leading from the front of the building to the stage proper. Backdrops usually show the surrounding countryside and often have a dominant central feature such as a pine tree or, quite frequently, Mount Fuji. Such scenes are particularly popular in travel-dances called *michiyuki,* such as the dance of Kanpei and Okaru from the story of *Chushingura.*

An example of an entire room setting may be seen in Act III, Scene II, "The Pine Room," from *Chushingura.* Such sets usually incorporate sliding doors at the rear which may be thrown open to reveal a further interior or sometimes a garden. In the famous play *Kuruwa Bunsho,* Izaemon throws open one door after another (each made smaller to achieve a perspective) as he appears to run through many rooms in search of his lover Yugiri.

One of the most spectacular sets involves the use of the large lift in the middle of the stage. In the play *Sanmon Gosan no Kiri* the robber Ishikawa Goemon is seen seated on the upper floor of the Nanzenji temple gate in Kyoto. The lift is then raised to reveal the entire gate and another character on the ground in front of it. This technique may be used in reverse to represent the collapse of a building as in the play *Masakado.*

Another spectacular change of set (which also incorporates the large lift) is seen at the end of the play about the famous gang of five thieves, *Benten Kozo.* After a long fight on a rooftop, Benten Kozo, to avoid capture, kills himself by plunging his sword into his stomach. As he begins to collapse, the scene is brought to an end by the entire roof, pulled by wires from the front, slowly turning over backwards on its axis to reveal its under-side which forms a backdrop as the lift rises to reveal the temple of the final scene (Fig. 17).

The revolving stage, known as the *mawari-butai,* had its first continual use in Japan and enables sets to be changed quickly to great effect. In the play *Nozaki Mura* (Nozaki Village) a typical cutaway village house is turned round through 180 degrees to reveal the rear which stands on a river bank. In *Kezori,* the story

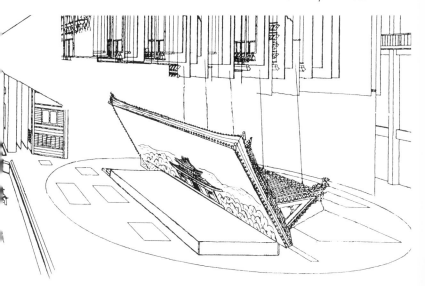

17. A modern Kabuki stage. Scene change at the end of *Benten Kozo*. The grille through which the *geza* musicians play is seen on the left front. The audience sits on either side of the *hanamichi.*

of a smuggler, a ship turns round so that its prow, on which the smuggler Kezori poses in a *mie*, points out into the audience.

Occasionally both the main stage and the *hanamichi* may be turned into the sea or a river by the use of very large sheets of cloth painted with waves. At the end of *Shunkan*, the story of an old man exiled on an island, the sense of isolation is heightened by the approach of the waves as Shunkan tries to follow the departing boat and is prevented by the incoming tide.

Special-effect properties are also cast as *o-dogu*, and these are mainly used for the appearance and disappearance of ghosts and for flying through the air. The most celebrated Japanese ghost story, *Yotsuya Kaidan*, uses several devices such as hidden trapdoors in the wall and a large wheel over which the actor rolls himself into view to effect a smooth, ghostly appearance.

Flying is known as *chunori* and has become the speciality of Ichikawa Ennosuke III, who has employed the device to great effect, particularly in his performance as Nikki Danjo in the play *Date no Ju Yaku* and as the fox Tadanobu in *Yoshitsune Senbon Zakura.* The character may either fly across the stage or out into the audience. The latter is achieved by a winch set up over the *hanamichi,* running from the main stage to the top of the third floor of the theater. Using a special costume under which a harness is concealed, the actor takes off near the main stage and rises up to the top floor, where he disappears into a specially constructed room in the seating area.

Ko-dogu (hand props)

By far the most important hand prop is the fan. There are many types of fans, depending on the uses to which they are put and on the time of year in which the play is set. The standard folding dance fan is called a *mai ogi,* while priests and characters in history dramas use a *chukei,* an old fan, the wooden slats of which are curved outward. Benkei in *Kanjincho* uses a *chukei.* Characters in plays set in the summer use the nonfolding flat fan called an *uchiwa.*

Swords are a vital prop in Kabuki, and there is an enormous variety, the use of which depends on factors such as the social status of the character. Samurai generally carry two swords, one short and one long, the longer being most commonly used in conventional sword fights. Certain swords are made so that the handguard will rattle when the sword is shaken. The class of characters called *go-chushin,* who run on to report the progress of a battle, often use this sword, the sound of which adds to the excitement as it is brandished through the air.

Characters played in the *aragoto* style, such as Umeomaru in *Kuruma Biki* (Fig. 26), sometimes carry three swords in keeping with their exaggerated costumes. The longest sword in Kabuki is the so-called *o-dachi* carried by Gongoro in *Shibaraku.* Its two meters are used to lop off the heads of about eight men at once!

Other hand props that are often seen include wads of paper, usually carried in the breast of the kimono; umbrellas made of oiled paper; small hand mirrors; large straw hats, ostensibly to keep off the rain but often serving to conceal the identity of the wearer; and lanterns such as the one held by Yuranosuke at the end of Act IV of *Chushingura.* The wad of paper has a variety of uses, and frequently women put the whole wad in the mouth at moments of great tragedy to suppress their cries of emotion. The wad may also be put in the mouth by men when inspecting a valuable sword to prevent the moisture from their breath from getting to the blade. A wad of paper is always carried by courtesans and has erotic connotations, being used in the more intimate moments of their profession.

De-dogu (small props)

The objects that surround the actor in a domestic setting are referred to as *de-dogu.* These include standing lanterns; charcoal braziers, known as hibachi, the only form of heating in premodern Japan; and tobacco boxes used in the lighting of the long Japanese pipes called *kiseru.* These pipes take a very finely powdered tobacco, which is smoked in a few puffs. Real pipes and real tobacco are usually used on the stage.

Other Props and Effects

Props that are destroyed in the course of each performance are referred to as *kiemono.* Examples include the saké cup and tray smashed in fury by Soga Goro in *Kotobuki Soga no Taimen,* the letter read by Yuranosuke and torn by Kudayu in Act VII of *Chushingura,* and the spectacular "spider's web," the *chisuji no ito,* thrown by the Earth Spider in *Tsuchigumo* (Fig. 6).

Nuigurumi refers to animal costumes, of which the most important is the Kabuki horse. The horse is played by two actors who must skillfully coordinate their leg movements to simulate those of the horse. Famous plays in which horses appear include *Ya no Ne* (The Arrowhead), the final act of *Chushingura*, and *Sanemori Monogatari* (The Tale of Sanemori), which contains a humorous moment when the horse refuses to move on. Another famous Kabuki animal is the wild boar (played by one man) in Act V, "The Musket Shot," from *Chushingura.*

Although characters in more realistic plays often sit on the floor, in stylized plays they actually sit on very low stools called *aibiki.* This makes them appear larger and also gives them more stage presence. When required to appear standing for long periods, actors also sit on tall *aibiki.*

In the days before electricity Kabuki was lighted either by daylight or by candles, and for certain plays this tradition is continued. For Izaemon's entrance in *Kuruwa Bunsho,* two black-dressed assistants *(kurogo)* precede and follow him carrying candles on the ends of long poles called *sashidashi.*

One final set of very important props are severed heads. These are made with varying degrees of realism, depending on the type of play. In *Shibaraku,* at the same moment that Gongoro severs the heads of about eight men with one blow of his great sword, assistants throw the heads across the stage. Amusingly, these are all attached to strings so that they can be gathered up easily. These heads are very simply painted, and similar ones are used for the famous "potato washing," *imo arai,* in the first act of *Yoshitsune Senbon Zakura.* Benkei throws some severed heads into an enormous water bucket and in a gesture of bombastic bravado, asking the audience to watch and enjoy the spectacle, proceeds to stir them around like potatoes.

The practice of identifying the head of an enemy severed in battle is known as *kubi jikken,* and heads for this, such as the one seen in *Moritsuna Jinya,* tend to be far more realistic. Such heads are usually kept in rather beautiful round boxes made of paulownia wood. The reaction of the character as he opens this box is inevitably one of the great moments in the drama.

Curtains

The use of the main stage and *hanamichi* curtains during a performance has been discussed earlier, in Chapter 2, but in addition to these there are a number of smaller curtains that have a variety of uses. The light blue *asagi maku,* a temporary drop-curtain, is revealed as the *joshiki maku,* the draw-curtain, is pulled aside. To increase the dramatic spectacle, the *asagi maku* is then dropped from above and is whisked from the stage, revealing the set. The black *keshi maku* is held by a black-dressed assistant to hide an actor's exit from the stage after having been killed, and the scarlet version is used to mask an entrance or costume change and then is whisked away for maximum dramatic effect. The *kasumi maku* is used in certain plays to hide the chanter and shamisen player before they are required to play. The black *anten maku* drops to conceal an entire set; and there are certain so-called *dogu maku* that are painted and used as introductory scenes before the main set is revealed. Finally, a special celebratory curtain may be seen for a *shumei,* the ceremony in which an actor takes a new, higher ranking name. These curtains are usually the gift of the actor's fan club or a department store and are decorated with his name and family crest.

CHAPTER 9

The Actors

 KABUKI HAS always been an actors' theater. Its humble beginnings on the dry bed of Kyoto's Kamo River gave rise to the derogatory term applied to early performers, *kawaramono,* or "objects of the riverbed." However, star actors quickly emerged who gained wealth and status far above their social class. In the Kyoto and Osaka region, Sakata Tojuro I (1647–1709) and in Edo, Ichikawa Danjuro I (1660–1704) were enormously popular and became role models for the increasingly wealthy merchant class.

Throughout the Edo period (1603–1868) the government tried to enforce a strict social hierarchy, but the wealth and popularity of Kabuki actors made this very difficult. Petty rules and regulations (such as a short-lived ban on gorgeous costumes) greatly restricted actors. Once, in the famous Ejima-Ikushima affair, when the court lady Ejima was caught dallying with the actor Ikushima, the total closure of Edo's Yamamura Theater was ordered. With the Meiji restoration in 1868, however, actors were freed of their social harness and eventually rose to a social status similar to that which is enjoyed by star actors everywhere today.

Kabuki Families and Shumei

Kabuki is an inherited profession, and although there is less pressure than in the past, the male children of star actors are still expected to follow in their fathers' footsteps and become Kabuki actors. Children usually make their debuts between the ages of five and eight and begin a long process, often lasting until middle age, of taking names of increasingly higher status until they achieve the highest rank open to them. This process and the ceremony that accompanies it is called *shumei.*

Although Kabuki actors have several names—a real name as a private citizen as well as a *yago,* or acting-house name—it is their stage name that is most important. In the case of the stage name Nakamura Utaemon VI, for example, Nakamura is the family name, Utaemon the forename, and VI means that he is the sixth person in Kabuki history to hold that name. It is usual, however, to refer to the actor only by his forename. The surname, known to all and common to many other actors, is omitted; and generation numbers are used only to refer to actors no longer performing. For clarity, however, I have retained the generation numbers throughout this book.

As in other traditional Japanese arts, Kabuki actors make their debuts as children; either by birth or adoption, they join one of the Kabuki "families." The most important families are Bando, Ichikawa, Ichimura, Kataoka, Matsumoto, Nakamura, Onoe, and Sawamura. A child will be given a low-ranking forename, and then, depending on the line open to him, will progress to names of higher rank.

Depending on the availability of a name, a *shumei* is usually decided by the actor's seniors and by the Kabuki management. The decision is announced to the Kabuki world, first of all in the press, and again a few months later in a special *shumei* performance in which the actor plays a leading role. If the name is of great importance, a formal stage announcement known as a *kojo* will also be part of the program.

In the late 1970s, actor Ichikawa Somegoro VI achieved fame and popularity in both Kabuki and other forms of theater, and even played the leading role in the musical *Man of La Mancha* in New York. In 1981, his ailing father, Matsumoto Koshiro VIII, decided to relinquish his high-ranking name to his son. In two months of celebratory performances at the Kabuki-za, Koshiro took the new name Hakuo I (he died a few months later) and his son became Matsumoto Koshiro IX. At the same time the grandchild rose to his father's old name and became Ichikawa Somegoro VII. These changes were announced to the audience daily in a *kojo* ceremony attended by all the actors appearing in the performances. Although Ichikawa Somegoro became Matsumoto Koshiro, his acting-house name *(yago)* Korai-ya remained the same. This can be somewhat complex, but a shared *yago* can, in fact, be a more reliable indication of family ties than is a common surname. Should an actor have several sons there may not be enough names available to go around, even a low-ranking one. In this case either a currently unused name from the past or the child's real forename may be used. This has occurred twice in recent years, with the late Onoe Tatsunosuke I, and again with Kataoka Takao I. An actor can keep a new name all his life, until he hands the name to his own son who then becomes *nidai-me*, "the second." Thus a new acting line is born. This was the case with Onoe Tatsunosuke I, who died in his early forties, and his own son has now become Tatsunosuke II.

A *shumei* can impose a great artistic burden on the actor, particularly if the new name has a long historical background. The succession to a new name can act as an inspiration as an actor achieves greater status and is given more important roles as he takes his turn in the continuation of a long tradition.

The best example of this continuing tradition is the acting line of Ichikawa Danjuro. The name Danjuro has very special significance in Kabuki. It is not only the oldest acting line, a number of its holders having been among Kabuki's finest actors, but the presence of a Danjuro has always held special meaning for the people of Edo and, later, Tokyo. The Edokko, "sons of Edo," have traditionally revered both the acting and the extravagant life styles of the early holders of the name, and look upon Danjuro as their own special actor. Although, as we shall see, there may be periods when a name remains in abeyance, there is a Danjuro performing at the moment who is the twelfth in the line. (There are some actors with higher generation numbers than twelve, the late Nakamura Kanzaburo XVII being one, but their early ancestors were theater managers rather than actors.)

On April 1, 1985, at the Kabuki-za in Tokyo, the actor Ichikawa Ebizo X succeeded to the name of Ichikawa Danjuro XII. The ceremonies and performances that celebrated this event were unprecedented in the history of Kabuki. The name Danjuro had been in abeyance since the premature death of Ebizo's father in 1965, and this event was seen as the rebirth of a tradition that would inject new life into the Kabuki world.

As part of his preparations to become Danjuro, Ebizo had to undergo several days of very severe religious austerities in the depths of winter at the temple of his family in Narita, near Tokyo. He also undertook a special pilgrimage to Narita, accompanied by over ten thousand of his fans and supporters, who traveled with him to pray for his success as the enormous responsibility of becoming the new Danjuro descended upon him.

Danjuro I, the founder of the line, made his debut in Edo at the age of thirteen. It was to complement his performance of superheroes that Danjuro invented the bombastic *aragoto* style of acting which became enormously popular with the people of Edo. He took the acting-house name of Narita-ya, having worshiped at the temple of Narita. Danjuro I met the ultimate end for an actor: He was stabbed to death during an on-stage fight scene by the actor Ikushima Hanroku.

Danjuro II (1688–1758) was the son of the first Danjuro and in time became equally popular. He was a versatile actor who created many of the plays that came to be adopted by the family as their speciality.

The third Danjuro (1721–42) died young. Danjuro IV (1711–78), said to be the son of Danjuro II, is credited with creating the role of Matsuomaru from the great classic play *Sugawara Denju Tenarai Kagami.*

Danjuro V (1741–1806), son of Danjuro IV, was considered one of the finest actors of his day and, unusually for actors in this line, often played female roles.

The sixth Danjuro (1778–99) also died young, but Danjuro VII (1791–1859), who lived during the final years of Kabuki's golden age, established forever the dominance of the line. He was as popular an actor as the first Danjuro, and at one point was banished from Edo by the government for living too extravagant a life style. He established the Danjuro collection of favorite plays known as the Juhachiban, and in 1840 gave the first performance of *Kanjincho,* a play derived from the Noh theater. His son, Danjuro VIII (1823–54), took the name when his father reverted to his old name of Ebizo, but despite his talent and popularity, he killed himself in Osaka.

Danjuro IX (1839–1903), together with Onoe Kikugoro V, led Kabuki through the troubled times of the Meiji restoration, beginning in 1868. The opening of the country and the questioning of traditional values could have led to the total destruction of Kabuki. Despite introducing many new ideas, however, Danjuro and Kikugoro can be credited with saving Kabuki for the twentieth century.

After the death of Danjuro IX the name remained in abeyance for many years until, in 1962, it was awarded to the eldest son of Matsumoto Koshiro VII. Born in 1909, he was very popular as Ichikawa Ebizo IX, but he felt he could not take the name without first honoring the student and son-in-law of Danjuro IX who had done much work in reviving the plays of the Juhachiban.

Therefore Ichikawa Sansho V (1882–1956) became Danjuro X posthumously, and Ebizo IX became Danjuro XI.

The present Danjuro was born in 1946 and actually made his debut under his real name of Horikoshi Natsuo and took the Kabuki name of Ichikawa Shinnosuke VI in 1958. He succeeded to the very high-ranking name of Ichikawa Ebizo X in 1969, and finally in 1985 he was judged by the peers and the Kabuki management to be worthy of the highest ranking name for a male-role actor and thus became Ichikawa Danjuro XII.

Even children who appear at first to have little talent will be led through the *shumei* system and may not, in fact, achieve greatness as actors. In this case the highest names will be withheld. However, there are many cases in which the award of a prestigious name actually has inspired an actor to new artistic heights.

A system of adoption also exists, and it is quite common for an actor with no male children to take the second or third son of another actor as his student, or *deshi*. Adoptions from outside the Kabuki world, however, are rare, although there is one notable exception in the present Bando Tamasaburo V. As a child, such was his skill in traditional dance that he was adopted by the great actor Morita Kanya XIV (1907–75) and is now his heir.

Not all Kabuki actors can be stars, of course, and there are many minor roles that must be filled by low-ranking actors known as *sangai yakusha*, or "third-floor actors," named for the old position of their dressing rooms in premodern theaters. Theoretically the same hereditary system exists for lower ranking actors, but in practice, possibly because they can never hope to achieve stardom, most minor actors now come from the school for Kabuki actors based in the National Theater in Tokyo. After graduating, a young actor will become the student of one of the master actors, who, in theory anyway, will continue to teach him his craft and guide his performances on the stage.

Although these actors often perform in minor roles, they also play a very important part both in the dressing room helping their master to dress and prepare, and on stage as stage assistants.

Koken and Kurogo (stage assistants)

In the play *Shibaraku* the main character, Kamakura Gongoro, enters along the *hanamichi* stage extension and delivers his famous name-saying speech. As he finishes he moves aside one of the great sleeves of his costume to allow a *koken*, an assistant formally dressed in the trousers and shoulder-wings costume called *kamishimo*, to bring him a drink of tea after the exertions of his speech. The actor may not, in fact, need to refresh himself, but the tradition prevails, and shows us the most formal side of the stage assistant's work.

Assistants may be either the formally dressed *koken* or the *kurogo*, who are dressed completely in black (*kuro*, in Japanese), including a black, see-through hood to cover the face. Their functions are often similar, but whereas the *koken*, although discreet, assists in full view of the audience, the *kurogo* crouches to make himself as small as possible—with anything black on the Kabuki stage being considered invisible.

Koken are seen most frequently in dances and dance-dramas, assisting an actor with adjustments to his costume, or handing or taking away small props such as fans, drums, or hand towels. During the spectacular quick costume changes called *hikinuki*, they move discreetly behind the dancing actor and remove the threads that hold the outer kimono together. At the precise moment they pull the kimono up from the shoulders to reveal the new costume and then hurry off, concealing the removed garment from the audience.

Koken also operate the butterflies on the ends of poles seen in the famous lion dance *Kagami Jishi*. In the dance *Ayatsuri Sanbaso*, in which the actor imitates a puppet, the *koken* assumes the role of puppeteer, occasionally untangling the imaginary crossed puppet strings.

In the most formal of the classic plays such as the Juhachiban, the *koken* is not only dressed in the *kamishimo* costume but also wears white makeup and a wig. If the assistant is a male-role player the wig will be dressed in a male style. If he is a female-role actor the wig style will be female. Although *koken* are usually minor actors, on special occasions a high-ranking actor may take this role and serve a younger one. Because of the auspicious nature of the *shumei* performances of Ichikawa Danjuro XII in 1985, the role of *koken* in *Shibaraku* was actually taken by Kataoka Nizaemon XIII, a very famous actor, then in his eighties and designated a Living National Treasure by the Japanese government.

The role of the *kurogo* is as important as that of the *koken*, but the *kurogo* is more discreet. He tries to hide himself from the audience as much as possible, crouching behind the actor to remove props or whisk away a stool, or *aibiki*, when it is no longer needed. *Kurogo* are also responsible for keeping the stage clear and removing any props that are no longer needed.

Although the world of Kabuki actors may seem feudal and even unfair, as potential talent has little or no chance to prove itself, the system has in practice served Kabuki well in its nearly four-hundred-year history. Appreciation of Kabuki as an abstract art is of little interest: Kabuki is the theater of its actors.

CHAPTER 10
The Audience

 KABUKI ACTORS have a very special relation-
ship with their audience. Kabuki is above all an
actors' theater, and the actor behind the role is
never forgotten. This actor-audience relationship
manifests itself in a variety of ways, from the *koen
kai*—fan clubs, similar to those of any Western
star—to far more subtle reminders of the actors' presence which
occur on stage and even during the course of a performance.

Kojo (a formal stage announcement)

During the course of a Kabuki performance, which will usually
consist of three or four plays, time may be set aside for the actors
to formally address the audience in a stage announcement called
a *kojo*.

The modern drop-curtain is raised to reveal one or more rows
of actors, all bowed with their heads to the floor, and dressed in
formal costume, with wigs and whitened faces. The male-role
actors wear wigs with the standard shaven crown and topknot,

18. *Sanbaso*. This auspicious dance traditionally was performed in the early morning at the beginning of a Kabuki performance. Sanbaso, Bando Mitsugoro IX.

19. The Nakamura-za theater, Third Month, 1800, by Toyokuni I. The play is an early version of *Shunkan*. Woodblock print triptych. Courtesy of the Trustees of the British Museum.

20. *Shibaraku*. The *genroku mie* pose. The sleeves, with the crest of the Danjuro line of actors, are held out by assistants. Kamakura Gongoro, Ichikawa Danjuro XII.

21. *Narukami.* The priest Narukami is seduced by Taema. Narukami, Ichikawa Danjuro XII. Taema, Nakamura Jakuemon IV.

22. *Kanadehon Chushingura*, Act IV. Hangan's *seppuku*. The dagger still in his stomach, Hangan motions to his retainer Yuranosuke that he wishes him to undertake the vendetta. Hangan, Onoe Baiko VII. Yuranosuke, Ichikawa Danjuro XII.

23. *Kanadehon Chushingura*, Act VI. Kanpei's *seppuku*. Kanpei kills himself believing he is responsible for the death of his father-in-law. Kanpei, Onoe Kikugoro VII. Okaya, his mother-in-law, Onoe Kikuzo VI.

24. *Kumagai Jinya*. Final scene. "Sixteen years of life—passed like a dream, like a dream." Kumagai, mourning the death of his son, gives up his life as a general to become a priest. Kumagai, Nakamura Kichiemon II.

25. *Kotobuki Soga no Taimen*. Final pose. Juro restrains his younger brother Goro from attacking Kudo Suketsune, who stands on the dais. (From third from left) Maizuru, Nakamura Jakuemon IV. Goro, Onoe

Tatsunosuke II. Juro, Onoe Kikugoro VII. Oiso no Tora, Nakamura
Utaemon VI. Kudo Suketsune, Ichimura Uzaemon XVII.

26. *Kuruma Biki.* The triplets in a *mie* symbolic of the tension between them. (From left) Sakuramaru, Nakamura Fukusuke IX. Matsuomaru, Ichikawa Sadanji IV. Umeomaru, Nakamura Hashinosuke III.

27. *Terakoya.* Matsuomaru completes the inspection of what is supposed to be the head of the young lord Kan Shusai but is in fact that of his own son. Matsuomaru, Kataoka Nizaemon XIII. Genzo, Ichimura Uzaemon XVII.

28. *Kasane*. Kasane's face becomes disfigured at the same spot at which her lover Yoemon drove a sickle into her father's skull. Kasane, Nakamura Shikan VII. Yoemon, Ichikawa Danjuro XII.

29. *Yotsuya Kaidan.* The body of the murdered Oiwa is washed up from a canal and begins to haunt her husband, Iemon. Oiwa, Nakamura Kankuro V. Iemon, Matsumoto Koshiro IX.

30. *Naozamurai. Sewamono* plays employ the realistic sets and costumes of the Edo period. Naozamurai (right), Bando Yasosuke V. Michitose, Nakamura Tokizo V.

31. *Seki no To.* The spirit of the cherry tree, Sumizome, prevents Kuronushi from cutting the tree down. Sumizome, Nakamura Utaemon VI. Kuronushi, Matsumoto Koshiro IX.

32. *Jiraiya no Danmari.* (From left) Ichikawa Danshiro IV, Nakamura Kankuro V, and Ichikawa Danjuro XII.

33. *Shinrei Yaguchi no Watashi*. The evil Tonbei is killed by a magical arrow. Tonbei, Ichikawa Danshiro IV. Ofune, Ichikawa Kamejiro II.

while the players of female roles, the *onnagata*, wear a wig dressed in a feminine style. An off-stage voice calls *"To-zai, To-zai!"* (East-west, East-west!), used as one would call "Hear ye!"; and with great formality the actors all raise their heads, face the applauding audience, and bow again. At this point the central, senior-ranking actor will rise again to introduce the *kojo*.

A *kojo* is usually held to announce an actor's succession to a new, higher ranking name, the so-called *shumei*, although occasionally it may commemorate a particular event such as the anniversary of the death of some great actor of the past. A *shumei kojo* is the most common, however, and the newly named actor will be introduced either by an elder relative or by a very high-ranking actor. All the other actors will then, in turn, raise their heads to add their congratulations. Finally the newly named actor, in language of great formality, asks the audience for its support and patronage and promises to do his best as he embarks on this new stage in his career. The senior actor then calls on all corners of the theater for support, and the actors again bow to the audience to bring the *kojo* to an end.

Occasionally a *kojo* may actually occur during the course of a play. This is often done when the child of a ranking actor is making his debut in one of the many *koyaku*, child roles. At a suitable moment the actors drop out of character, kneel before the audience, introduce the child, and ask for the continuation of the audience's patronage. The formalities over, the leading actor will then say, "Well, let us get on with the play!" and the performance will continue.

The *shumei kojo* of the Ichikawa Danjuro line of actors is the most formal of all, and at the end of the *kojo* the new Danjuro is presented with a congratulatory scroll on a small wooden stand and is called on to demonstrate his skill at *nirami*, the furious crossed-eye pose seen in a *mie*. Still kneeling, he lifts the stand in his left hand, stamps forward his right foot, makes a fist of his right hand in front of his chest, and crosses one eye over the other in a *mie* pose, to the accompaniment of the wooden *tsuke*

Bando
Hikosaburo

Bando
Mitsugoro

Bando
Tamasaburo

Ichikawa
Danjuro

Ichikawa
Danshiro

Ichikawa
Ennosuke

Ichikawa
Monnosuke

Ichikawa
Sadanji

Ichimura
Uzaemon

Iwai
Hanshiro

Kataoka
Gado

Kataoka
Nizaemon

34. Actors' crests

clappers. Danjuro holds this pose as the *kojo* ends to great applause and shouts from the audience.

Mon (actors' crests)

Another manifestation of the way in which actors make their presence felt to the audience are the family crests, or *mon*, which are often seen on the actors' costumes and props.

Kawarasaki
Gonjuro

Matsumoto
Koshiro

Nakamura
Ganjiro

Nakamura
Jakuemon

Nakamura
Kankuro

Nakamura
Kichiemon

Nakamura
Shikan

Nakamura
Tokizo

Nakamura
Tomijuro

Nakamura
Utaemon

Onoe
Baiko

Onoe
Kikuguro

Onoe
Tatsunosuke

Sawamura
Sojuro

Sawamura
Tanosuke

Sawamura
Tojuro

Most Japanese families have a crest which may be displayed on kimono for formal occasions such as weddings. For a Kabuki actor the crest is very important and is often seen both on stage and in the dressing room. In the play *Shibaraku* the great crests of interlocking rice measures on the sleeves of the hero's costume remind us that this play is one of the famous eighteen favorite plays of the Ichikawa family, the Juhachiban, and is really their property. Usually, however, an actor displays his own crest either on his costume or on a hand prop.

During the dance *Musume Dojoji* the actor coyly holds the center of a hand towel, known as a *tenugui*, in his mouth and then opens the towel out to display to the audience his own personal crest. Later in the play the dancer and the priests who watch the dance will interrupt the drama to throw some of these towels imprinted with the crest out to the audience as souvenirs of the occasion. The formally dressed stage assistants, the *koken*, may also display this crest on their costume.

Certain roles have their own crest which takes precedent over that of the actor. In the fourth act of *Kanadehon Chushingura*, all the sliding doors in the mansion of Enya Hangan are decorated with his personal crest of crossed feathers.

The crests of the actors can be clearly seen on stage during a *kojo* stage announcement. The actors all appear in the formal *kamishimo* costume of wide trousers and shoulder wings, the lapels of which are decorated with their personal crests. The *mon* is a constant reminder to both actor and audience of an actor's family and acting tradition which may go back over two hundred years.

Kakegoe (calls from the audience)

By far the most extraordinary connection between the actor and his audience are the calls made by certain members of the audience from the top floor of the theater.

In Kabuki the moment of greatest tension is often the point of least physical action. This is called *ma*, meaning a pregnant pause. It is most obvious in the *mie* poses which are an important feature of many Kabuki plays. All action ceases and the music stops as, at the climax of the *mie*, the actor poses and glares. It is at this point, much to the surprise of first-time visitors to Kabuki, that several men on the top floor of the theater may shout out to the actor as a form of appreciation and applause known as *kakegoe*.

Kakegoe (literally "calling-voice") has its roots in the *home kotoba*, or words of praise, in which a fan of earlier times would stand at some point during the play and deliver a speech in praise of his favorite actor. This practice probably died out some hundred and fifty years ago, but there remained a tradition of the plebeian audience shouting out the names of favorite actors during the play.

These random shouts gradually became more organized and integrated into the actors' pauses, filling in the *ma* and creating a new and exciting dimension. Actors, too, began to appreciate *kakegoe*. As the timing became more critical, the injected calls served to fill the pause, aiding the actor by supplementing his own inner tension. Today actors greatly appreciate skilled *kakegoe* and miss it when they perform before a foreign audience.

The calls are mostly of the actors' *yago* or generation number. *Yago* is a difficult word to translate but is really a name associated with an acting family tradition or an acting "house." All actors have a *yago* name which ends in *ya*, a syllable that in Japanese has a shop or business connotation. Actors with the same *yago* come from the same acting family. As we have seen earlier, Ichikawa Danjuro has the *yago* of Narita-ya, which stems from a family connection with the temple at Narita. Ichikawa Ennosuke, despite having the same surname, has the *yago* of Omodaka-ya; and the Onoe Kikugoro acting line is of the house of Otowa-ya. (A list of actors and their *yago* may be found in the Appendix, p. 159.) As actors progress they succeed to newer, higher ranking names, and so their generation number may also be called out to them as *kakegoe*. The present Danjuro is the twelfth *(juni)*, to hold that name, so one may hear *"Junidai-me!"* (The twelfth!). Ennosuke is the third *(san)*, so for him *"Sandai-me!"* (The third!) will be shouted. Occasionally other things may also be called to the actors such as *"Matte 'mash'ta!"* shouted at a famous moment during the play and meaning "That's what I've been waiting for!" Such calls, however, are not heard often. Calls are commonly made at entrances and exits and at points of *ma* during the play. These may either be *ma* in speech or, in the case of a *mie* pose, for example, *ma* in movement. These calls require the most skill and precise timing so that the caller integrates with, and does not disturb, the actor.

Any knowledgeable member of the audience may call out, but there are groups of so-called professionals who, despite the name, are not paid but have a pass to the theater in order to perform this service for actors and create atmosphere for the audience. These men are known as *o-muko-san* because they call from the position formerly occupied by the plebeian audience—the rear, cheap seats of the theater, most distant *(muko)* from the stage.

Kakegoe, when performed well, can greatly aid the actor in his performance and create a lively atmosphere for the audience. Kabuki without *kakegoe* is lacking in the vitality that this extraordinary and unique contact between actor and audience demonstrates.

CHAPTER 11

Backstage

 A FEW YEARS ago I purchased an *oshiguma* face-pressing (see Chapter 7, p. 86) which had been taken by the great female-role actor Nakamura Utaemon VI. As part of the deal, which was in support of an actors' charity, Utaemon also agreed to sign the back of the picture when it had been framed, and arrangements were made for me to take the *oshiguma* to his dressing room for the signing. I entered through the hanging curtain at the door and, removing my shoes, stepped up onto the tatami mats. Passing by a row of five or six suitably humble students, I was ushered into his presence.

Utaemon, one of the most venerable of Kabuki actors and designated a Living National Treasure by the Japanese government, is generally regarded as one of the greatest female-role players in the history of Kabuki. Kneeling on a cushion with his back to his mirror, he bowed in greeting—not the bow of a Japanese man, with hands together to the front, but the bow of a Kabuki princess, hands on either side of the body, pointing backward, head demurely bowed to one side. In the high-pitched voice which is totally natural to him, he said, *"Utaemon de gozaimasu."* (I am Utaemon.) I had entered a world that would not have been out of place in the feudal Japan of two hundred years ago.

In Western theaters the dressing room or backstage area is sacrosanct, to be intruded upon only by the closest friends of the actor, and even then only after, and not before, the performance.

The dressing room of the Kabuki theater, the *gakuya* as it is called in Japanese, is a totally different world, still to be entered with care but one that reflects the feudal society of premodern Japan which still, to a degree, exists in the world of Kabuki actors.

In the beginning, during the early development of the Kabuki playhouse, the *gakuya* was a large covered area directly behind the stage which all actors shared. As the buildings became larger and more permanent, two further stories were added, and these also served to segregate the actors. Male-role actors used the first (ground) floor, nearest the stage; female-role players, the *onnagata,* took the second floor; and the players of supporting roles became "third-floor actors," *sangai yakusha,* a term by which they are still referred to.

The present Kabuki-za in Tokyo follows this layout, although the old distinction between the male- and female-role players no longer exists. The best *gakuya* are still considered to be those nearest the stage, although in fact there are only four large rooms on this floor of the Kabuki-za. These will be used by the stars in any particular month and will usually be reserved for the most venerable actors. Some of the larger *gakuya* have their own baths, but most actors will use the communal bath.

The individual rooms are entered through a hanging curtain called a *noren,* decorated with the actor's name and family crest. The rooms are divided into two areas. The vestibule, or *genkan,* common to all Japanese homes, is where visitors leave their shoes before stepping up on to the tatami matting, and this area usually has small washing and cooking facilities. It is here that the actor's helper, known as a *tsukebito*, usually a young woman, will do odd jobs and make tea for any guests. The only strange thing about this *genkan* is that above the shoes, on the wall, hangs a sword rack.

The *gakuya* proper is larger, and the actor kneels on a cushion in front of a lighted mirror. From here he greets his guests and, when the time comes, he will begin his makeup. The morning program begins at 11:00 A.M. and the evening performance usually finishes around 9:30, so the actor may need several costumes throughout the long day. Some of these will be brought in from the costume room, while others may be seen hanging up in the dressing room itself. If he has been playing a male role that requires *kumadori* makeup, he may have been taking *oshiguma* face-pressings, and these will be pinned up along the wall to dry. The actor may share his dressing room with his son, if he is appearing, and there will also be, depending on his status, between one and five or six students, his *deshi*, who will help the actor to dress and prepare. When he has finished dressing, the wig dresser, the *toko-yama*, will bring in the freshly dressed wig and help the actor put it on. Preparations complete, the actor leaves the dressing room for the stage.

Although practice varies, it is common for actors to have many visitors during the day who may come to watch them dress and make up. Visitors tend to be members of the actor's fan club, admitted by the club's secretary to exchange a few words and watch these preparations. The actors have an amusing phrase for outsiders who are continually seen backstage, *gakuya suzume*, which means "dressing-room sparrow." A minor actor who walks around backstage with an air of great importance is called a *gakuya* Danjuro, after the line of great actors.

Apart from the fans, a continual stream of people come and go. Managers and officials on business, and others, who enter no further than the *genkan*, come merely to greet the actor. The first greeting in the Kabuki theater, at whatever time of day, is *"ohayo gozaimasu!"* which in the Japanese world outside means merely "good morning." Lower ranking actors, some dressed in their street clothes, others already in costume, enter, say *"ohayo gozaimasu!"* and leave. The callers who shout from among the audience also greet the actors in the same way, and at the end of the day the process is repeated with the words *"otsukare sama!"* —"You must be very tired!"

Gifts such as green tea, cakes, or chocolate are also brought in return for a minor favor, while at other times far more substantial rewards may be given in exchange for an *oshiguma*, for example.

The backstage bustles with an atmosphere of excitement and preparation, and a feeling of the feudal world of premodern Japan can still be experienced in the Kabuki *gakuya*.

CHAPTER 12

At a Rehearsal

ALTHOUGH MOST visitors to Kabuki will not have the opportunity to see a rehearsal, watching actors prepare their performance is a fascinating experience. While Kabuki appears rather static, with productions differing from one another in only minute detail, plays are nevertheless thoroughly rehearsed before the beginning of the monthly run.

Until well into the nineteenth century, Kabuki was more fluid than it is today. It was common for three authors to contribute to a single drama, and different actors also molded and formed characters and plays. Great playwrights such as Chikamatsu Monzaemon, Tsuruya Nanboku, and Kawatake Mokuami created many of Kabuki's major dramas, but despite their contributions, the concept of a sacrosanct text did not exist. Many alterations were made, and plays were handed on by word of mouth.

In modern times scripts have been written down, and diligent research by scholars has led to the production of authentic, annotated editions of Kabuki plays. Today, actors regularly receive a script, called a *daihon*, in the early stages of their preparation. For well-known plays such as *Kanjincho* or *Terakoya* the *daihon* may be needed only as a reminder to the actor. In recent years, however, there have been many revivals of forgotten plays, notably by Ichikawa Ennosuke III and by the National Theater of Japan, which pursues a policy of producing plays as near as possible to their original form. For many of these, the lost text has had to be rewritten and a *daihon* is a necessity.

After the initial read-through, and assuming the play is from the standard repertoire, rehearsals proper begin in the period between one month's run and the next. A program at the Kabuki-za begins on the first day, called *shonichi*, usually the first of the month, and ends on the last day, known as *senshuraku*, about the twenty-fifth. The three days before the opening of the new program are a period of intense rehearsals, beginning at ten or eleven in the morning and lasting well into the evening or even night. A rehearsal of a revival by Ennosuke has been known to begin at 11:00 A.M. on the thirty-first of the month and end one hour before the 11:00 A.M. opening performance the following day.

Assuming that there may be eight different plays in one month's performance, they will all be rehearsed during these three days.

The plays will all be given a main rehearsal in full costume on the stage but are also run through without costume. Regular Kabuki audiences will be surprised to learn that in the absence of a proper rehearsal room in the Kabuki-za, these rehearsals take place in the lobby, with the souvenir-stalls moved to one side. The actors taking part in these run-throughs wear traditional kimono or, in the summer months, lightweight *yukata*, and make use of only small hand props such as fans. The musicians appear with the actors, seated on the thin reed matting that is laid over the lobby carpet.

The main stage rehearsal, the *butai-geiko*, is normally a

complete run-through with the actors in full costume, although very rarely an actor may perform in costume but without makeup or wig. This is usually due to lack of time, as he may have to rehearse several plays on the same day. Much time is spent at *butai-geiko* by the set builders, especially if the play is a rarely performed one. The actors and musicians are usually well enough prepared by this time for only minor timing problems to require any attention; and only the elaborately choreographed fight scenes, the *tachimawari,* which may involve large numbers of actors, need any repetitions.

While rehearsals take place in the lobby and on the stage, actors awaiting their turn wander around the theater, sometimes watching from the seats, sometimes smoking, chatting, or practicing their golf strokes! Some may sit in the auditorium in full costume and makeup, and it is fascinating to try to recall the days when the whole audience must have resembled them with their samurai hairstyles and Edo-period costumes. Minor actors greet their superiors with the ubiquitous *ohayo gozaimasu!,* either dropping to their knees if they are on the stage or just touching the carpet with one hand if they are in the lobby. In return they usually receive a slight nod of the head.

Ichikawa Danjuro XII, now in his forties but the holder of one of Kabuki's most illustrious names, enters the auditorium along the *hanamichi* from backstage. He is in full costume for an *aragoto* role and is followed by a retinue of about six assistants. Behind him comes a young girl holding a fan and a small box with his cigarettes and a drink, and behind her comes an assistant dressed in the all-black costume of a *kurogo,* carrying an *aibiki,* a stool that magically appears beneath Danjuro as soon as he begins to sit down. Seated, he greets fellow star Onoe Kikugoro VII, whom he has known and performed with since they were children, and as it is warm, the girl begins to fan him. It is hot beneath the costume, wig, and makeup. Eventually the set is complete and the actors take up their positions for the rehearsal, which will usually be run through with hardly a hitch.

Although various officials of the theater may be responsible for the set and lighting (which in Kabuki is usually fairly constant), the real director of the play is the leading actor who may be either performing himself or teaching the play to a less senior actor. He will ensure that not only his own role but also those of the supporting actors are performed exactly in accordance with tradition. Such things as an actor's position on stage or the timing of a particular movement are all done within the confines of the *kata*, the form or model, dictated by tradition, and which the actor must follow. It is common for an older actor, for example, to remind a younger one of how his father or uncle may have performed a certain section. Age and rank are paramount, and even an actor of the status of the present Nakamura Shikan VII, now in his sixties, may be given quite a difficult time if he does not perform exactly as his uncle, Utaemon VI, wishes.

Finally, if a dance is being rehearsed, a high-ranking dance teacher will always attend the rehearsal of even the most venerable actors to correct or refine any minor points that may occur. In practice most things will have been discussed long before the stage rehearsal, but should any refinements be required, the actor, however senior, always defers to the teacher.

CHAPTER 13

At a Performance

 THE FOLLOWING is an account of one of Kabuki's most famous plays in performance. I have attempted to describe the scene, including stage directions and timing, and the effect of the climaxes and high points on the audience. For most of the play I have provided a synopsis of what is said, although I have also included a certain amount of translation. This account is based on an actual performance—given for the *shumei* (succession) of Ichikawa Danjuro XII in April 1985. The cast was as follows:

ROLE	ACTOR	YAGO
Musashibo Benkei	Ichikawa Danjuro XII	Narita-ya
Yoshitsune	Onoe Baiko VII	Otowa-ya
Retainers	Kataoka Gato V	Matsushima-ya
	Nakamura Kankuro V	Nakamura-ya
	Ichikawa Sadanji IV	Takashima-ya
	Bando Minosuke VII	Yamato-ya
Togashi no Saemon	Nakamura Kanzaburo XVII	Nakamura-ya
Swordbearer & three guards		

Kanjincho (The Subscription Scroll) is regarded as one of the finest plays in the Kabuki repertoire. A dance-drama, it was first performed by Ichikawa Ebizo (better known for most of his career by the name Danjuro VII) in 1840, being an adaptation of a much older Noh play called *Ataka.*

The story is set in the world of the Heike-Genji civil wars and concerns the plight of the young Lord Minamoto Yoshitsune, about whom so much Japanese literature and legend are concerned. Yoshitsune is fleeing to the north to escape the soldiers of his jealous older half-brother, the Shogun Yoritomo, who wishes to capture and kill him. He is traveling with his right-hand man Benkei and four of his generals, who are all dressed as members of the warrior-priest sect known as *yamabushi.* Benkei was actually a priest before entering Yoshitsune's service and was probably a real *yamabushi.* Yoshitsune himself is disguised as their porter. Their path to the north is blocked by several barriers that have been set up by Yoshitsune's brother to stop him. Their first barrier is at Ataka, and it is here that the action takes place. The set is the simple backdrop of the great pine tree, and the musicians who perform in the *nagauta* style appear in formal costume, kneeling and seated on platforms at the rear of the stage.

KANJINCHO

The play is about to begin, and from behind the curtain we hear the plaintive sound of the flute with drum accompaniment. As *Kanjincho* is a dance-drama the usual Kabuki draw-curtain is not used for the opening. A drop-curtain is raised to reveal the simple set of a great pine tree painted on the plain backdrop. The musicians are seated in two rows along the rear of the set.

The striped curtain incorporated into the left side of the stage set is raised on poles from the bottom corners, and the actor Nakamura Kanzaburo XVII in the role of Togashi enters, followed by his swordbearer and guards. Kanzaburo is greeted by shouts of "Nakamura-ya!", his acting-house name, and *"Ju-shichidai-me!"* (The seventeenth!) called out to him as a form of appreciation by the *kakegoe* callers among the audience at the top of the theater.

He directly faces the audience, and in the formal language typical of the Noh theater he announces his name, Togashi no Saemon. He says that he is in command of this barrier gate. This formal style of directly addressing the audience comes from the Noh theater and is preserved in this Kabuki adaptation. Togashi and his men have been warned by Yoritomo that his younger half-brother Yoshitsune is trying to make an escape to the north via the Ataka barrier. He and his followers are reported to be disguised as *yamabushi* priests and therefore all *yamabushi* are to be stopped and interrogated.

Togashi's guards say that they have only recently put some dubious *yamabushi* to death. Should any more come their way they will immediately be bound and taken before Togashi.

Togashi tells them to be careful and apprehend all *yamabushi*. They must serve their lord in Kamakura (i.e., Yoritomo) well.

He finishes his speech and is again applauded with shouts of "Nakamura-ya!" Togashi turns to take up his position on the right of the stage, seated on a black lacquer barrel, facing left, which the audience is to understand as the barrier. The flute and drum music at this point are in the style reminiscent of the Noh theater. The cries of the drummers are an integral part of their performance. The singers begin and the solemn lyrics refer to the dew-drenched sleeves of the traveling *yamabushi* priests.

The singers and musicians now prepare us for the entry along the *hanamichi* of Yoshitsune and his retainers. Yoshitsune and his men have escaped from Kamakura and are now traveling to the north, a path that must take them through the Ataka barrier.

Shouts of "Otowa-ya!", the acting-house name of Onoe Baiko VII, greet his appearance in the role of Yoshitsune. His pure white face indicates his aristocratic background, but he is dressed as a mere traveling porter. Because of his gentle nature Yoshitsune is often played by an *onnagata*, female-role player, and Baiko is one of the most famous veteran *onnagata* actors. Yoshitsune poses, looking up at the surrounding mountains, and stops on the *hanamichi*, facing right, directly into the audience, to await his men. We are to understand that they are now very near the barrier.

His followers enter in turn, though it is the last to enter, the warrior-priest Benkei, who has the main role in this play. Legend says that Benkei fought and was defeated by Yoshitsune on the Gojo Bridge in Kyoto and since that time has been a devoted follower of the young lord, protecting him with his great strength and courage.

Benkei enters, played by Ichikawa Danjuro XII. Ichikawa Ebizo X has, in the month of this performance, succeeded to the very illustrious name of Danjuro, and his first appearance on the stage as the new Danjuro is now greeted with much applause and shouts of "Narita-ya!" and *"Junidai-me!"* (The twelfth!) from the *kakegoe* callers. Although Yoshitsune's generals are all disguised as *yamabushi,* Benkei is dressed differently from the others, his costume being finer and more striking.

Yoshitsune, turning to Benkei, tells him that their path to the north is now blocked by this barrier. He had wished to take his own life rather than be put to death by some anonymous guard, but he has adopted Benkei's suggestion of disguising himself as a porter in the hope of passing through. He asks the others about their chances of getting through the barrier.

The first general says he would prefer to fight his way through. They have swords, why should they not use them? The next two men also wish to try to fight their way through, and if necessary they will defend their lord with their lives rather than submit to the guards. The final, older, and wiser general, however, says nothing.

Benkei, who has listened passively to their words now interrupts them, telling them to wait *("Shibaraku!, Shibaraku!")*.

He warns them of the rashness of trying to fight their way through. They may well succeed in getting through this one gate, but there are many more to follow and the news of their deed would quickly spread. He fears that Yoshitsune's disguise has already become known, and he apologizes for the humiliation of dressing his lord as a humble porter. He suggests that he should try to talk their way through the barrier and that Yoshitsune, feigning exhaustion, should hide his face under his hat.

Yoshitsune agrees to the plan and orders them all to obey Benkei. Benkei passes them on the *hanamichi* and leads them to the barrier.

They now move off the *hanamichi* onto the main stage and Benkei goes forward to confront Togashi and his men. Yoshitsune crouches on the ground, facing the audience but with his hat covering his face.

Benkei tells them that they are *yamabushi* and that they wish to pass through the barrier. The guards, however, order them to halt, and they alert Togashi to their presence.

Benkei explains that they are collecting funds for the rebuilding of the great Todaiji temple in Nara and that they have been ordered to travel north in their quest. They must pass through this barrier. Togashi replies that although their purpose is commendable, no *yamabushi* may pass through.

The rising tension between them is indicated by the beating and calls of the drummers. Benkei asks why they may not pass, and as Togashi prepares to explain his reasons, both he and Benkei turn and directly face the audience. Their turn at this point, indicative of the tension between them, is greeted by calls of "Nakamura-ya!" and "Narita-ya!" In the tradition of Noh, they continue to face the audience even though they are talking to each other.

Togashi tells him that the younger half-brother of Yoritomo has fled from Kamakura and that he is reported to be traveling north disguised as a *yamabushi* priest. Therefore this roadblock has been set up to catch him. The speech is punctuated by the beats of the *ko-tsuzumi* and *o-tsuzumi* drums. The guards confirm Togashi's words and say that although there are many *yamabushi*, not one will pass through the barrier.

Benkei replies that their orders concern false priests, not real *yamabushi* like them. The guards say that all *yamabushi* are suspect and that only yesterday they put three to death.

"Well, was one of the heads that of Yoshitsune?" asks Benkei. Togashi, actually quite disturbed at the order to put holy men to death, says, "That is a difficult question . . . but no one will pass!" He turns away from the audience and resumes his seat to the right of the stage.

Benkei is outraged by this treatment. He turns to his men, however, and tells them that they will die bravely and that they should gather round to perform their last rites.

The first short dance section follows. The shamisen begin a short, repeated rhythmic pattern as Benkei retires to the rear of the stage where the *koken* assistants adjust his costume for the dance. Yoshitsune remains where he is while the four generals form a square in the center of the stage for their final prayers. His preparations complete, Benkei takes up his position in the middle of the group of four and the singers begin.

They comment on their devotion to the deity of the *yamabushi*, the fearsome god Fudo Myoo, saying that they have achieved enlightenment and will be reborn into Buddhahood. Those who inflict death on the *yamabushi*, however, will be damned. In the course of the short dance Benkei makes obeisances to their god, and they all rub their Buddhist rosaries together in prayer. It is unlikely at this point that Benkei is really going to give in so easily. He is going through a performance in order to test Togashi's determination.

Togashi is indeed unnerved by this seeming willingness to die. If they really are collecting for the Todaiji temple, he asks, then they must have a *kanjincho*, and he would like to hear it. A *kanjincho*, the subscription scroll of the play's title, was a list of subscribers to a religious cause which began with a pious exhortation to contribute money or gifts. It was written in extremely florid and difficult religious language.

Benkei is momentarily thrown by this request, because of course they have no such *kanjincho*. He decides on the desperate ploy of improvising a *kanjincho* text from an unused scroll which they have in their possession. Because of the complexity of the language employed in these texts, such an improvisation would have been difficult in the extreme.

The musicians comment on the desperate situation and the fact that they have no such *kanjincho*. We come now to one of the most famous scenes in Kabuki and a great test of the actors' abilities. The retainers move back to the left of the stage and Benkei, receiving the scroll from a *koken*, circles the stage, showing the rolled-up scroll to Togashi. He stops in the middle of the stage, Togashi on the right and Yoshitsune still seated on the left. He slowly unrolls the scroll and with great formality holds it out and begins to read.

As Benkei begins to read, Togashi, already suspicious, gradually rises and edges toward Benkei to see if there really is anything written on the scroll. As the same time, (usually unobserved by the majority of the audience) Yoshitsune, aware of the tense situation, peers out at them from under his hat.

One of the great moments in Kabuki follows. Benkei becomes aware of Togashi and must act quickly. Suddenly, accompanied by a high-pitched squeal from the flute, he stamps his foot and pulls the scroll tightly to his breast. Togashi, knowing that he has been caught in the act of trying to look at the scroll, quickly turns to the audience and Yoshitsune again hides his face under his hat. The *kakegoe* callers erupt with shouts of "Narita-ya!", "Nakamura-ya!", and "Otowa-ya!", the acting-house names of Danjuro, Kanzaburo, and Baiko. The calls, entering as they do at random, one upon the other and in canon, greatly add to the tremendous drama of the moment. The pose that the three adopt is the first of the *mie* in the play and is called the Tenchijin—

"Heaven, Earth, Man"—Mie after the respective positions of Benkei, Yoshitsune, and Togashi.

Although nothing in the text confirms this, most actors, including the present Danjuro, feel that Togashi has managed to see the scroll and now knows that Benkei is bluffing. Yoshitsune is definitely with them. From now on he baits Benkei to see how far Benkei is prepared to go in trying to deceive him as he carries on reading the scroll.

He completes the reading and performs the second of the *mie* poses. The deity of the *yamabushi*, and also that of the Danjuro line of actors, is the god Fudo Myoo, who is always depicted holding a rope with which he binds and hauls souls to their salvation and with an upturned sword with which he severs them from carnal desire. Substituting the scroll for the sword and his rosary for the rope, Benkei poses in this position.

Togashi is satisfied with the reading but now says he wishes to know more of the *yamabushi* sect. The following section of the play is called the "Yamabushi Mondo" (Yamabushi Interrogation). Togashi questions Benkei about the *yamabushi* priesthood in language that is extremely difficult to understand and replete with obscure religious references. With regard to actual esoteric Buddhism, this section is very accurate and the references are correct. I will not, however, attempt to explain them here, but will give the whole "Yamabushi Mondo" in a fairly accurate translation which conforms roughly to the actual length of the questions and answers. Although there is little action, the drama lies in the rising tension between Benkei and Togashi as the questions and answers become more and more intense.

TOGASHI: There are many sects of the priesthood, but why is it that the appearance and practices of the *yamabushi* are so fierce?

BENKEI: To free the world from evil, the *yamabushi* must tread steep and dangerous paths, repelling beasts and serpents which cause harm in the world. We show compassion to man, and through religious austerities we force ghosts and spirits to attain enlightenment. Sweeping away evil, we pray for peace, but devils are intimidated by our stern and solemn appearance. The 108 beads of our rosary symbolize the 108 passions of man.

TOGASHI: What is the meaning of your costume and hat?

BENKEI: The hat and robes are like the armor of the warrior. We carry the sword of Amida and staff of Shakyamuni to travel the length and breadth of the world.

TOGASHI: All priests carry a staff, but the staff which you carry, the *kongotsue*, you use as a weapon. Why is that?

BENKEI: The staff is divine and was first used by the hermit Arara when he practiced austerities in India. He taught the young Buddha and kept the staff by his side in times of hardship.

TOGASHI: Why was it adopted by the *yamabushi*?

BENKEI: Our founder Ennoshokaku used it to cross mountains and plains, and we inherit it from him.

(The interrogation now becomes more intense as Togashi tries to trick Benkei. Their speech becomes quicker.)

TOGASHI: You are priests but you carry swords. Are they for show, or do you use them?

BENKEI: Although they seem the bow and arrow of a scarecrow, our swords are not just for show. We strike all who violate the law of Buddha—beasts, serpents, and men.

TOGASHI: You cut that which you can see, but what of formless demons who obstruct the path of Buddha?

BENKEI: For that we use the nine sacred syllables.

(The tension increases further, and they gradually edge toward each other.)

TOGASHI: What of your costume?

BENKEI: It takes the shape of Fudo Myoo, our deity.

TOGASHI: The meaning of your hat?

BENKEI: The five wisdoms and twelve laws of karma.

(The tempo and tension increase.)

TOGASHI: Your surplice?

BENKEI: The color of the Kue Mandala.

TOGASHI: Your leggings?

BENKEI: The blackness of the Taizo world.

TOGASHI: Your eight-laced sandals?

BENKEI: The eight-petaled lotus seat of Buddha.

TOGASHI: The air we breathe in and out?

BENKEI: Ar and Un, two characters.

TOGASHI: What is the meaning of the nine sacred syllables?

(This is the most difficult question of all, and Togashi, furious that he is unable to trick Benkei, screams the question, saying, *"Nan to? Naaan to?!"* (What is it? What is it?!) The callers shout out "Nakamura-ya!" and *"Jushichidai-me!"* in appreciation of Kanzaburo's performance as we reach this climax. Togashi has failed to shake Benkei and he must now decide to kill them all, including the man he knows to be Yoshitsune, or let them go— with terrible consequences to himself.)

BENKEI: *(in contrast to the preceding section, speaking slowly and deliberately)* That is the innermost secret of our religion, but to dispel your doubts I shall tell you. The nine syllables are Rin, Pyo, To, Sha, Kai, Chin, Retsu, Zai, Zen. When you say them, stand upright and strike your teeth together thirty-six times. With the thumb of your right hand trace four vertical and five horizontal lines. At the same time intone Kyu Kyu Nyo Ritsu Ryo, and all forms of evil will disappear like frost under boiling water and you become invincible against all enemies.

Benkei concludes by saying that if Togashi has any more questions he will be glad to answer them. He calls on the gods to bear witness to the truth of his words and then performs the next *mie* pose. He stamps his left foot forward, the rosary in his left hand he holds in front of him, and the scroll in his right he holds high, level with his head. This is the so-called *genroku mie*. The audience applauds the *mie* and the *kakegoe* callers shout "Narita-ya!" and *"Junidai-me!"* in appreciation, and here ends the "Yamabushi Mondo."

Togashi seems thoroughly broken by Benkei's performance. He has reached a terrible decision and has decided to let them pass. He says that he is now satisfied and he too wishes to make a contribution to their collection for the Todaiji temple. The singers describe the gifts that Togashi makes as his men bring them forward and place them in the center of the stage.

Benkei thanks him and says that he will surely be honored by the gods for his gifts to the temple. He blesses the gifts with his rosary and, realizing that they may come in useful, he says they will take the two bags of gold now and pick up the rest when they return from the north. He tells his men that they must now go on their way, and the singers sing of their happiness at being allowed through the barrier.

As they begin to move off toward the *hanamichi,* however, one of the guards rushes to Togashi and points out the figure of the porter. Togashi, whatever his private reasons for allowing them to pass, is forced to stop them. He throws his fan aside and an assistant helps him to lower the right sleeve of his outer robe in preparation for a fight. Taking his sword, he shouts at them to stop.

Benkei on the *hanamichi* rushes to restrain his men, as a fight would give them away for certain. He mimes with his hand for them to remain where they are and, stamping his feet in determination, he returns to the center of the stage to confront Togashi. Yoshitsune again seats himself center stage with his hat over his face.

When Benkei demands to know why the porter had been stopped, Togashi says that he "looks like a certain person."

"Looks like a certain person?" asks Benkei incredulously, and he demands to know what Togashi means.

Togashi explains that one of the guards thinks he looks like the Hogan Dono, the formal title of Yoritomo's half-brother Yoshitsune.

Again Benkei is forced to take drastic action. He rounds on the porter and berates him for his slowness and stupidity in holding them back from their path to the north. How dare he resemble such a noble lord as Yoshitsune!

Benkei is forced to adopt one final desperate strategy. To convince Togashi that this really is a porter, he decides to strike him. For Benkei to strike his own lord, however, would be an unforgivable act in any circumstances. He raises his staff above his head and, pausing momentarily, closing his eyes in horror at what he is about to do, he symbolically strikes Yoshitsune's head and sweeps him aside to the rear of the stage.

Togashi still refuses to allow them to pass, and Benkei accuses the guards of wanting to steal their funds. The two groups now confront each other in the next dance section. Yoshitsune's men rush to join Benkei, but he motions them to restrain themselves and holds them back with his outstretched staff. As Benkei desperately tries to stop his men from open confrontation, the guards form themselves up behind Togashi and the two groups edge together, meeting in the middle of the stage. The audience applauds and shouts ("Narita-ya!" "Nakamura-ya!") as, in dance steps, the two groups alternately advance and retreat from each other. Finally Benkei, twirling his staff, clears the center of the stage and brings the dance to a close.

If Togashi has any further doubts, he threatens to beat the porter to death.

Benkei's action has amazed Togashi. He is now in no doubt whatever that the porter is Yoshitsune, and understands full well what it meant for Benkei to strike his lord. He begs Benkei to desist and decides to let them pass even though it will mean he will have to take his own life in atonement.

The following short scene is regarded as one of the great moments in the play. Togashi hands his sword to his swordbearer, and assistants help him to put back on the sleeve of his robe. He pauses, slowly looking across at Benkei. Suddenly, appalled at what has happened, he closes his eyes, tilts back his head in horror, and quickly leaves the stage by the small door in the right-hand corner of the set. The callers shout "Nakamura-ya!" and *"Jushichidai-me!"* in appreciation as Kanzaburo is regarded as one of the greatest exponents of this role. (Kanzaburo died, aged 78, in 1988.)

The scene that follows is highly regarded for its mood of somber pathos which contrasts with the drama of the rest of the play. Yoshitsune and his men have now passed through and are a short distance from the barrier. Yoshitsune reconciles himself with the distraught Benkei.

His hat no longer necessary, Yoshitsune emerges from behind his retainers and takes up his position to the right of the stage. The face of the actor Baiko is again visible, and the *kakegoe* callers greet him with calls of "Otowa-ya!" One by one the generals take up their positions along the rear of the set. They are greeted in turn by calls of their *yago:* Minosuke, "Yamato-ya!"; Kankuro, "Nakamura-ya!"; Sadanji, "Takashima-ya!"; and Gato, "Matsushima-ya!" Finally Benkei, whose costume has been adjusted at the rear of the set, also turns and takes up his position opposite Yoshitsune. He too is greeted by calls of "Narita-ya!" (The calls for this section should be fewer and more restrained, befitting the somber nature of the scene. The shamisen music, too, is slow and plaintive.)

Echoing his first words at the beginning of the play, Yoshitsune asks, *"Ika ni Benkei?"* (Well, Benkei?) He thanks Benkei profoundly for what he has done. No ordinary man could have brought them through the barrier safely without the wit and courage that he has shown.

The generals too speak of the day's events. The first says that today was surely the most dangerous they have experienced. The next says that Hachiman, the god of war, must be protecting their lord, and he urges them to continue on their way. The third says how deeply grateful they are to Benkei; and the fourth, too, praises Benkei's great courage.

Benkei gives thanks for their good fortune. He tells them how

35. *Kanjincho.* Having struck Lord Yoshitsune in an attempt to convince Togashi that he is a mere porter, Benkei and his men confront Togashi

and the guards in a dramatic dance sequence. Benkei (left), Ichikawa
Danjuro XII. Togashi, Onoe Kikugoro VII.

he has great strength, but when he came to lift the staff to strike his lord his arm went numb. He is greatly moved that his lord is willing to pardon such an action.

A solo singer joins the shamisen and tells us that for the first time in his life Benkei shed tears at the thought of his lord's generosity. Yoshitsune edges forward to him and extends his hand in friendship ("Otowa-ya!"). Benkei looks up and, seeing the gesture, is overcome with emotion. He retreats along the ground and bows his head to the floor ("Narita-ya!"). Yoshitsune, also overcome, covers his eyes with this hand. (The audience applauds.)

Born into this warrior's life, Yoshitsune says, he was devoted to his brother. Now he will sink like a ship, lost in the western sea. He bemoans the fate that has estranged him from his brother and led to his flight.

Benkei tells of the hardships of a samurai's life and now begins a dance in which in mime he describes some of the sea battles they have fought together.

He rests his head on his arm in fatigue as the singers describe how little time they had for sleep while on the waves.

He rows the boat, holding the fan as an oar. He extends the fan to indicate a high precipice and turns it upside down to represent the mountains where they could hardly see for the falling snow.

With his fan, he again mimes the mighty waves at Yashima, the site of one of the great battles that led to Yoshitsune's defeat of the Heike clan. He mimes releasing an arrow at the height of the battle. Benkei concludes the dance with the *ishinage no mie,* performed in the pose representing the throwing of a stone. (Unusually, this is the first *mie* in this play that is accompanied by the beating of the wooden *tsuke* clappers.) At this vigorous climax the *kakegoe* callers applaud with shouts of "Narita-ya!" and *"Junidai-me!"*

He counts on his fingers their three years of victories before misfortune befell them. In sorrow, the generals hide their tears with their hands. They all bow to Yoshitsune and prepare to continue their journey.

Suddenly they are interrupted by the voice of Togashi calling for them to wait. Yoshitsune quickly resumes his disguise with his hat covering his face.

Togashi and his men again enter through the Noh-style curtain on the left of the stage. He apologizes to them for the trouble he has caused and says he has come to offer Benkei a drink of saké. The men bring the saké and cup forward and as the host, Togashi drinks first.

They place the cup before Benkei and he thanks Togashi. Two of Togashi's men, each bearing flasks of saké, seat themselves on either side of Benkei in order to fill his cup. (This drinking scene provides a final moment of light relief before the dramatic ending of the play. The plaintive musical accompaniment at this point is of great beauty, provided by a solo singer and shamisen.)

With great formality, Benkei lifts the cup and drinks. They immediately offer him more, but as a great drinker, he finds the cup too small and motions for them to bring him the lid of the lacquered barrel which earlier was used as Togashi's seat.

Together they fill the lid with drink, and taking a deep breath, Benkei blows away the alcohol fumes before drinking.

Now a little drunk, Benkei begins to enjoy himself. The singers tell of his one and only love for a woman. For the benefit of the guards he counts the single occasion on his fingers and points as if a beautiful woman were close at hand. When the guards look for her he slaps them on the back and they roll over with the strength of his blow. Benkei bursts into a fit of laughter ("Narita-ya!").

To the amazement of the guards he carries on drinking, but when he motions them to give him even more, they refuse. He feigns anger and, afraid of him, they hand over the flasks for him to pour for himself. He drinks again, and the singers tell of his love and that he cannot achieve enlightenment in the "floating world" of pleasures. Drinking the last sip, he lifts the lid higher and higher until he ends up wearing it as a hat ("Narita-ya!"). The lid is actually held in place over his head by a *koken*.

The mood of the music becomes more lively, and Benkei stands and begins a staggering, drunken dance. He mimes the old game of floating a wine cup down the stream. As it passes, the catcher must drink its contents and compose a poem before the next cup arrives. Benkei throws his fan to represent the cup.

In mime, he scoops up the waters of the pure mountain stream and turns to Togashi, offering to dance for him.

The isolated drumbeats and the calls of the drummers remind us again of the Noh theater as we come to the final climax of the play. Benkei now performs a dance of longevity, the famous "Ennen no Mai." In the chanting style of Noh he begins to recite the words of the dance, wishing Togashi a long life.

The singers tell us that Benkei was a real priest and would have been familiar with the auspicious dance. He again recites words from the dance and looks up at a waterfall, miming the water with his fan. The singers tell of the roar of the water and the rays of the sun that shine down in unending light.

Still dancing but aware of the ever-present danger, Benkei subtly motions with his fan to Yoshitsune and his men to leave quickly. To cries of "Otowa-ya!" and applause from the audience, Yoshitsune and his generals hurry out of the scene along the *hanamichi*.

Benkei straps on his back the portable altar which they brought with them, and bowing to Togashi, he prepares to follow them. The singers say that he feels as though he has stepped on the tail of a tiger and escaped the jaws of a poisonous serpent. He moves toward the *hanamichi* and Togashi comes to the center of the stage. First stamping each foot in turn, Benkei bangs his staff to the ground and the *ki* clappers are struck in a single *chon* beat signaling the end of the play ("Narita-ya!" "Nakamura-ya!"). Turning back to Togashi, who now has no option but to take his own life, the two of them perform a *mie* pose as the Kabuki *joshiki maku* striped curtain is run across the stage and then held back so that the *geza* musicians can see Benkei on the *hanamichi.*

Benkei is left alone on the *hanamichi* in total silence, but the excited audience bursts into applause and for the next thirty seconds there are intermittent shouts of "Narita-ya!" and *"Junidai-me!"* As well as the *kakegoe* callers, members of the audience may also shout at this point and we may hear cries of *"Matte 'mash'ta!"* (This is what I've been waiting for!) along with other expressions a great deal less formal, to the delight of the audience. Benkei looks along the *hanamichi* to see that his lord is progressing safely, and then he solemnly turns toward the stage and bows to the absent Togashi, who he realizes has let Yoshitsune escape. He turns and faces the auditorium, looking up at the audience seated high above him and out into the stalls. He closes his eyes and bows, and once more the audience bursts into applause and calls. As an actor, Danjuro expresses his gratitude at having come to the end of the play, and as a character Benkei lowers his head in relief at the ordeal past.

We come now to the most famous exit in Kabuki, for which the whole audience has been waiting. To the accompaniment of the *tsuke* beaters, Benkei twirls his staff into position under his left arm and performs the final grand *mie* of the play ("Narita-ya!" *"Junidai-me!"*). To great applause he bounds off along the *hanamichi,* hopping on one leg and then the other in the famous *tobi roppo,* the flying exit, in which his arms are said to fly in six directions—north, south, east, west, to heaven, and to earth. The curtain is drawn completely across the stage and the musicians finish playing. As soon as Benkei is gone the audience begins to leave the auditorium. Kabuki actors do not take curtain calls.

CHAPTER **14**

Where to See Kabuki

KABUKI TRAVELS abroad often, and in one year there is good chance of seeing a performance in one of the major cities of Europe or America.

If you want to be sure of seeing Kabuki, however, you must travel to Japan. Although Kabuki does tour throughout the country, the center of the Kabuki world is still Tokyo. Tokyo has two major Kabuki theaters: the Kabuki-za, the present building of which dates from 1951; and the National Theater of Japan, the Kokuritsu Gekijo, which opened in 1966.

The Kabuki-za
Ginza 4-12-15, Chuo-ku, Tokyo.
Normal ticket bookings can be made by telephone:
(03) 3541-3131.

The Kabuki-za is situated directly above Higashi-Ginza subway station on the Hibiya Line, about a five-minute walk from the central shopping district of Ginza. From the cheapest seats in this theater you will not be able to see the *hanamichi* at all, but you will have the secret pleasure of knowing that together with the *kakegoe* callers, the most knowledgeable of all Kabuki fans, you will know when the actor has entered by the "swish" sound of the curtain rings!

Performances at the Kabuki-za usually run from the 1st to the 25th, and there is a morning (usually from 11:00 A.M. to 4:00 P.M.) program and an evening (4:30 to 9:00 P.M.) program in which different plays are performed. If you wish to attend the whole day you will need two tickets.

There is a wide range of ticket prices. Those for the better parts of the first and second floors are comparable to prices for good seats at first-run shows in London and New York theaters. Tickets for third-floor seats are considerably less. And there is also a special fourth floor, where, for a fraction of the regular ticket price, you can see just one play or one act of a play which, in full length, takes the whole day. This floor is called the *maku mi,* and tickets for it go on sale about fifteen minutes before the play begins. You will have to check with the theater for the exact times. Even if the theater is completely sold out it is nearly always possible to see a play from this floor. The English-language Earphone Guide is not available here, however. Once you are on this fourth floor and decide to stay for the next play or act, it is not necessary to go back down to the ticket office. The attendant can sell you another ticket on the fourth floor.

The National Theater of Japan (Kokuritsu Gekijo)
Hayabusa-cho 4-1, Chiyoda-ku, Tokyo
Telephone: (03) 3265-7411

The National Theater is right across from the Imperial Palace and just down the road from the British Embassy. The nearest station is Nagatacho, on the Yurakucho subway line.

Even from the cheapest seats of the National Theater one has a good view of the *hanamichi,* and this theater has the largest revolving stage in the world, with an impressive array of other lifts and traps which allow for some spectacular changes of set. For many people, however, the modern National Theater, for all its facilities, is somewhat lacking in the atmosphere and lively bustle which used to typify the theaters of old Edo.

Performances at the National Theater usually begin on about the 4th or 5th of the month and finish around the 25th or 26th. This theater is dedicated to all the Japanese performing arts, and Kabuki is not performed every month. There are two theaters, the large theater and the small theater; Kabuki is usually, but not always, performed in the larger one.

Performances usually begin around 12:00 P.M., and on two days a week there is a matinee and an evening performance, which usually begins at about 5:00 P.M.

You are advised to buy tickets in advance if possible, as this theater is smaller than the Kabuki-za and is often sold out. If you have to buy a ticket on the day of the performance, try to arrive at least an hour before the performance begins. If possible, telephone first to check availability. Someone at the box office should be able to speak English. Ticket prices are comparable to those of the Kabuki-za, except that there is no *maku mi* section for viewing just parts of the program.

Other major theaters in Japan where Kabuki is occasionally performed:

TOKYO: **Shimbashi Embujo.** Very near the Kabuki-za. Tel. (03) 3541-2211

KYOTO: **Minami-za.** Tel. (075) 561-1155

OSAKA: **Naka-za.** Tel. (06) 211-1566

Shin Kabuki-za. Tel. (06) 631-2121

NAGOYA: **Misono-za.** Tel. (052) 211-1451

Earphone Guide

I must now declare my interest and say that as one of the

narrators, I really wish that all visitors to Kabuki, either in Japan or abroad, would use the Earphone Guide. Although it is widely used by most members of the audience, it is very discouraging to see people who do not take it, knowing that they are missing at least half of Kabuki's interest and enjoyment, available for a very small cost.

The company that runs the service has been producing a guide in Japanese since about 1976 and decided to begin a similar guide in English for foreign visitors. The guide is not a simultaneous translation but provides essential comments and explanations about the plot, music, actors, and other features of Kabuki which may be difficult to understand.

The guide is prepared in time for the dress rehearsal and is done by the narrators themselves, who must first of all read the script and decide exactly how much translation is necessary for a full understanding of the play. When this is in place, other comments about aspects and features of Kabuki may also be explained, depending on the time available, but without disturbing the on-stage action or turning the guide into a lecture.

The comments, which can range in number from about 60 to over 300 depending on the length of the play and style of the narrator, are then recorded and an operator sits in the theater for every performance, following a script and starting and stopping the taped comments on cue.

The Earphone Guide is available at both the National Theater and the Kabuki-za. The same company usually produces a guide for most foreign tours.

Appendix: List of Kabuki Actors

The following is an alphabetical list of major actors. It is not a complete list, and I apologize to the many fine lower ranking actors whom I have left out. Included are the actors' *yago*, or acting-house names, and family relationship where I consider them to be important. Actors may change their names in the course of their careers, but this list is accurate at the time of publication.

Actor's name	Born	Yago	Family relationship
Bando			
Hikosaburo VIII	1943	Otowa-ya	First son of Uzaemon XVII
Mitsuguro IX	1929	Yamato-ya	
Shonosuke I	1954	Otowa-ya	Third son of Uzaemon XVII
Tamasaburo V	1950	Yamato-ya	Adopted son of Morita Kanya XIV (d. 1975)
Yajuro I	1956	″	
Yasosuke V	1956	″	Son of Mitsugoro IX
Ichikawa			
Danjuro XII	1946	Narita-ya	Son of Danjuro IX (d. 1965)
Danshiro IV	1946	Omodaka-ya	Younger brother of Ennosuke III
Danzo IX	1951	Mikawa-ya	
Ennosuke III	1939	Omodaka-ya	Elder brother of Danshiro IV

Actor's name	Born	Yago	Family relationship
Kamejiro II	1975	″	Son of Danshiro IV
Komazo XI	1957	Korai-ya	
Monnosuke VIII	1959	Takino-ya	
Otora III	1967	″	Son of Sadanji IV
Sadanji IV	1940	Takashima-ya	
Shinnosuke VII	1977	Narita-ya	Son of Danjuro XII
Somegoro VII	1973	Korai-ya	Son of Matsumoto Koshiro IX
Ichimura			
Manjiro II	1949	Tachibana-ya	Second son of Uzaemon XVII
Uzaemon XVII	1916	″	
Iwai			
Hanshiro X	1927	Yamato-ya	
Kataoka			
Gato V	1935	Matsushima-ya	First son of Nizaemon XIII (d. 1994)
Hidetaro II	1941	″	Second son of Nizaemon XIII
Nizaemon XV	1944	″	Third son of Nizaemon XII
Roen VI	1926	″	
Takataro I	1968	″	Son of Nizaemon XV
Kawarasaki			
Gonjuro III	1918	Yamazaki-ya	
Matsumoto			
Koshiro IX	1939	Korai-ya	Elder brother of Kichiemon II
Nakamura			
Baigyoku IV	1946	Takasago-ya	Adopted son of Utaemon VI
Fukusuke IX	1960	Narikoma-ya	First son of Shikan VII
Ganjiro III	1936	″	″
Hashinosuke III	1965	″	Second son of Shikan VII
Jakuemon IV	1920	Kyo-ya	
Kanjaku V	1959	Narikoma-ya	First son of Ganjiro III
Kankuro V	1955	Nakamura-ya	Son of Kanzaburo XVII (d. 1988)
Kantaro II	1981	″	First son of Kankuro V
Karoku V	1950	Yorozu-ya	Elder brother of Kasho III
Kasho III	1956	″	Younger brother of Karoku V
Kichiemon II	1944	Harima-ya	Younger brother of Koshiro IX

Actor's name	Born	Yago	Family relationship
Matagoro II	1914	″	
Matsue V	1948	Kaga-ya	Adopted son of Utaemon VI
Senjaku III	1960	Narikoma-ya	Second son of Ganjiro III
Shibajaku VII	1955	Kyo-ya	Second son of Jakuemon IV
Shichinosuke II	1983	Nakamura-ya	Second son of Kankuro V
Shinjiro I	1959	Yorozu-ya	Younger brother of Tokizo V
Shikan VII	1928	Narikoma-ya	Nephew of Utaemon VI
Tokizo V	1955	Yorozu-ya	Elder brother of Shinjiro I
Tomijuro V	1929	Tennoji-ya	
Tozo VI	1938	Kaga-ya	
Utaemon VI	1917	Narikoma-ya	
Onoe			
Kikugoro VII	1942	Otowa-ya	Son of Baiko VII (d. 1995)
Kikuzo VI	1923	″	
Matsusuke VI	1946	″	
Tatsunnosuke II	1975	″	Son of Tatsunoke I (d.1987)
Ushinosuke VI	1977	″	Son of Kikugoro VII
Otani			
Tomoemon VIII	1949	Akashi-ya	First son of Jakuemon IV
Sawamura			
Sojuro IX	1933	Kinokuni-ya	Elder brother of Tojuro II
Tanosuke VI	1932	″	
Tojuro II	1943	″	Younger brother of Sojuro IX

For Further Reading

Adachi, Barbara C. *Backstage at Bunraku*. Tokyo: Weatherhill, 1985.

Bowers, Faubion. *Japanese Theatre*. New York: Hermitage House, 1952. Tokyo: Tuttle, 1974.

Brandon, James R., ed. *Chushingura*. Honolulu: The University Press of Hawaii, 1982.

Brandon, James R., trans. *Five Classic Plays*. Cambridge: Harvard University Press, 1975

Brandon, James R., William P. Malm, and Donald H. Shively. *Studies in Kabuki: Its Acting, Music, and Historical Heritage*. Honolulu: The University Press of Hawaii, 1977.

Brandon, James R., and Tamako Niwa. *Kabuki Plays: Kanjincho and the Zen Substitute*. New York: Samuel French, 1966.

Dalby, Liza. *Geisha*. Tokyo: Kodansha International, 1983.

Dunn, Charles J., and Bunzo Torigoe, trans. and ed. *The Actors' Analects: Yakusha Rongo*. Tokyo: Tokyo University Press, 1969.

Ernst, Earle. *The Kabuki Theatre*. Revised ed. Honolulu: The University Press of Hawaii, 1974.

Gunji, Masakatsu. *Kabuki*. Tokyo: Kodansha International, 1986.

——. *The Kabuki Guide*, translated by Christopher Holmes Tokyo: Kodansha International, 1987.

Halford, Aubrey S., and Giovanna M. Halford. *The Kabuki Handbook*. Tokyo: Tuttle, 1956.

Japan Culture Institute. *Great Historical Figures of Japan*. Tokyo, 1978.

Kawatake, Mokuami. *The Love of Izayoi and Seishin.* Translated by Frank Motofuji. Tokyo: Tuttle, 1966.

Keene, Donald. *Chushingura: The Treasury of Loyal Retainers.* New York: Columbia University Press, 1971. Tokyo: Tuttle, 1981.

Leiter, Samuel. *The Art of Kabuki: Famous Plays in Performance.* Berkeley: The University of California Press, 1979.

——. *Kabuki Encyclopedia.* Westport, Connecticut: Greenwood Press, 1979.

Malm, William P. *Japanese Music.* Tokyo: Tuttle, 1959.

——. *Nagauta: The Heart of Kabuki Music.* Tokyo: Tuttle, 1963.

Nitobe, Inazo. *Bushido: The Soul of Japan.* Tokyo: Tuttle, 1969.

Reischauer, Edwin O. *Japan: The Story of a Nation.* New York: Alfred A. Knopf, 1974. Tokyo: Tuttle, 1981.

Richie, Donald, and Miyoko Watanabe, trans. *Six Kabuki Plays.* Tokyo: Hokuseido Press, 1963.

Sansom, G. B. *Japan: A Short Cultural History.* London: Cresset, 1952. Tokyo: Tuttle, 1981.

Scott, A. C., trans. *Genyadana: A Japanese Kabuki Play.* Tokyo: Hokuseido Press, 1953.

——. *The Kabuki Theatre of Japan.* Tokyo: Tuttle, 1955.

——. *The Puppet Theatre of Japan.* Tokyo: Tuttle, 1963.

Seidensticker, Edward. *Low City, High City.* New York: Alfred A. Knopf, 1983. Tokyo: Tuttle, 1983.

——. *Tokyo Rising.* New York: Alfred A. Knopf, 1990. Tokyo: Tuttle, 1990.

Seward, Jack. *Hara-kiri.* Tokyo: Tuttle, 1968.

Shaver, Ruth M. *Kabuki Costume.* Tokyo: Tuttle, 1966.

Yoshida, Chiaki. *Kabuki: The Resplendent Theater of Japan.* Tokyo: The Japan Times, 1977.

The following Japanese titles are included for those readers with the necessary knowledge who may wish to delve deeper into Kabuki. Even those who do not read Japanese may find some of the titles of interest as many of them are copiously illustrated.

Bando, Mitsugoro. *Kumadori.* Tokyo: Haga Shoten, 1969. *Kumadori* makeup.

Gunji, Masakatsu, ed. *Kabuki Juhachiban.* Tokyo: Shueisha, 1979. The Juhachiban collection of plays.

Hattori, Yukiyo. *Ichikawa Danjuro.* Tokyo: Heibonsha, 1978. The history of the Danjuro line of actors.

Hattori, Yukiyo, Tetsunosuke Tomita, and Hirosue Tamotsu, ed. *Kabuki Jiten*. Tokyo: Heibonsha, 1983. A comprehensive encyclopedia of Kabuki.

Ichikawa, Ennosuke. *Kabuki Koza*. Tokyo: Shinchosha, 1984. Explanations of Ennosuke's stage tricks.

Ishii, Masako, and Tomoko Ogawa. *Danjuro Nidai*. Tokyo: Kodansha, 1990. Photographs of Danjuro XI and XII.

Kawatake, Toshio, ed. *Genshoku Kabuki Shosai*. Tokyo: Grafsha, 1982. Informative, detailed photographs.

Koyama, Kanoh. *Kabuki Kanshogaku Nyumon*. Tokyo: Kobun Shuppankan, 1991.

——. *Kabuki no Zatsugaku*. Tokyo: Grafsha, 1983.

——. *Kotengeino no Kisochishiki*. Tokyo: Sanseido, 1983.

Matsuda, Seifu. *Kabuki no Katsura*. Tokyo: Engeki Shuppansha, 1986. Drawings of all Kabuki wigs.

Nakamura, Tetsuro. *Seiyojin no Kabuki Hakken*. Tokyo: Gekishobo, 1982. Early foreign views of Kabuki.

Nishikata, Setsuko. *Nihon Buyo no Sekai*. Tokyo: Kodansha, 1988. The world of Japanese dance.

Tomoyama, Haruo. *Shumei Zen Kiroku. Junidai-me Ichikawa Danjuro*. Tokyo: Heibonsha, 1985. Photographs of Danjuro XII and his *shumei* performances.

Usui, Kenzo. *Ebizo Kara Danjuro Made*. Tokyo: Shueisha, 1985. Photographs of Danjuro XII and his *shumei* performances.

Index of Actors, Plays, and Roles

Only the most common English titles of plays are included here. Other titles are either very obscure when rendered into English or, as in the case of *Narukami*, are also the name of the principal character. The plays of the Juhachiban are marked with an asterisk. The three great classic plays of Kabuki are *Kanadehon Chushingura, Sugawara Denju Tenarai Kagami*, and *Yoshitsune Senbon Zakura*. "*Kuruma Biki*" and "*Terakoya*" are two acts of *Sugawara Denju Tenarai Kagami* that often are performed separately. Roles are shown indented following the plays.

Ataka, Noh play, 31, 136
Ayatsuri Sanbaso, 102
Bando: Minosuke VII, 135; Tamasaburo V, 16, 101
Benten Kozo (Benten the Thief), 36, 59, 76, 83, 90
    Benten Kozo, 90
Chushingura. See *Kanadehon Chushingura*
Date no Ju Yaku, 92
    Nikki Danjo, 92
Fudo*, 39
Funa Benkei (Benkei in the Boat), 29
Fuwa*, 39

Gedatsu*, 39
Hiragana Seisuiki, 64
    Matsuemon, 64
Horikoshi Natsuo: real name of Ichikawa Danjuro XII, 101
Ichikawa Danjuro acting line: 98, 121, 125, 142; Danjuro I, 20, 44, 84, 96, 99; Danjuro II, 33, 44, 100; Danjuro III, 100; Danjuro IV, 100; Danjuro V, 100; Danjuro VI, 100; Danjuro VII, 31, 38, 44, 100, 136; Danjuro VIII, 100; Danjuro IX, 20, 86, 100; Danjuro X, *See* Ichikawa Sansho V; Danjuro

XI, 101; Danjuro XII, 16, 38, 44, 99, 101, 103, 126, 133, 135, 141, 142, 153

Ichikawa: Danshiro IV, 16; Ebizo IX, 100, 101; Ebizo X, 99, 101, 138; Enno I, 38; Ennosuke III, 16, 92, 125, 126, 132; Sadanji IV, 43, 135; Sansho V, 101; Shinnosuke VI, 101; Somegoro VI, 98; Somegoro VII, 98

Ichimura: Uzaemon XV, 72; Uzaemon XVII, 88

Ikushima Hanroku, 99

Imoseyama Onna Teikin (An Example of Noble Womanhood), 35

Jayanagi*, 39

Jiraiya no Danmari, 37

Kagami Jishi (Lion Dance), 60, 78, 102
  butterflies, 102

Kagekiyo*, 39

Kamahige*, 39

Kanadehon Chushingura (The Treasury of Loyal Retainers), 25, 33, 34, 37, 48, 57–58, 67, 75, 81, 83, 90, 93, 94, 124
  Banni, 48
  Enya Hangan, 57–58, 81, 124
  Kanpei, 37, 58, 67, 83, 90
  Ko no Morano, 48, 81
  Kudayu, 93
  Oboshi Yuranosuke, 34, 93
  Okaru, 67, 90

Kanjincho* (The Subscription Scroll), 25, 29, 31, 32, 33, 38, 39, 44, 45, 62–63, 64, 71–72, 78, 92, 100, 132, 135–153
  Benkei 25, 45, 62–63, 64, 71–72, 92
  Togashi no Saemon, 32, 62
  Yoshitsune, 72

Kan'u*, 39

Kataoka: Gato V, 135, 147; Nizaemon XIII, 103; Takao I, 98

Kenuki* (The Tweezers), 39
  Kumadera Danjo, 39

Kezori, 90–91

Kirare Yosa (Scarred Yosa), 83

Koi Bikyaku Yamato Orai (Love's Courier on the Yamato Highway), 35, 57

Kotobuki Soga no Taimen (The Auspicious Confrontation of the Soga Brothers), 33–34, 93
  Asahina, 34
  Kudo Suketsune, 34
  Soga Goro 33-34, 93
  Soga Juro 33-34

Kumagai Jinya (Kumagai's Camp), 35

Kuruma Biki (Pulling at the Carriage), 47, 92
  Sakuramaru, 47
  Shihei, 47
  Umeomaru, 47, 92

Kuruwa Bunsho (Love Letters from the Licensed Quarter), 35, 46, 47, 90, 94
  Izaemon, 35, 47, 90, 94
  Yugiri, 35, 47, 90

Kyoganoko Musume Dojoji. See *Musume Dojoji*

Masakado, 90

Matsumoto: Hakuo I, 98; Koshiro VII, 100; Koshiro VIII, 98; Koshiro IX, 16, 72, 98

Meiboku Sendai Hagi, 34, 59, 83
  Masaoka, 59, 83
  Senmatsu, 59

Migawari Zazen (The Zen Substitute), 32

Miyajima no Danmari (Danmari at Miyajima), 37, 65

Momijigari (The Maple Viewing), 78

Morita Kanya XIV, 101

Moritsuna Jinya (Moritsuna's Camp), 35, 94

Musume Dojoji (The Maiden at Dojo Temple), 30, 38, 59, 62, 78, 124
Hanako, 62

Nakamura: Kankuro V, 16, 135, 147; Kantaro II, 59; Kanzaburo XVII, 59, 71, 99, 135, 136, 147; Kichiemon II, 16; Nakazo I, 30; Shikan VII, 134; Utaemon V, 72; Utaemon VI, 13, 16, 97, 127–128, 134

Nanatsumen*, 39

Naozamurai, 72

Narukami*, 39
Taema ,39

"*Ninokuchi Mura*" (Ninokuchi Village) act of *Koi Bikyaku Yamato Orai*
Magoemon, 57

Nozaki Mura (Nozaki Village), 90

Onatsu Kyoran, 59

Onoe: Baiko VII, 16, 135, 137; Kikugoro V, 20, 38, 100; Kikugoro VI, 71, 73; Kikugoro VII, 71, 133; Tatsunosuke I, 98; Tatsunosuke II, 98

Oshimodoshi* (Devil Pusher), 38

Ren Jishi (Double Lion Dance), 78

Sagi Musume (The Heron Maiden), 73

Sakata Tojuro I, 20, 46, 96

Sanemori Monogatari (The Tale of Sanemori), 94

Sanmon Gosan no Kiri, 90
Ishikawa Goemon, 90

Seki no To (The Osaka Barrier), 30

Shibaraku* (Wait!), 39, 43, 44, 47, 70, 86, 87, 92, 94, 102, 103, 124
Kamakura Gongoro, 43–45, 70, 85, 92, 94, 102
Takehira, 43, 47
Yoshitsuna, 43

Shinrei Yaguchi no Watashi, 65
Tonbe, 65

Shunkan, 34, 76, 81, 83, 91
Chidori, 83
Seno, 81

Sonezaki Shinju (Love Suicide at Sonezaki), 35

Sugawara Denju Tenarai Kagami (Sugawara's Secrets of Calligraphy), 34, 48, 57, 100. See also *Kuruma Biki*; *Terakoya*
Matsuomaru, 100
Shirataya, 57

Sukedakaya Kodenji II, 43

Sukeroku Yukari no Edo Zakura* (Sukeroku and the Cherry Blossoms of Edo), 38, 42, 57, 68, 69, 72, 78, 83
Agemaki, 42, 70, 83
Ikyu, 57, 70, 72
Sukeroku (Soga no Goro), 24, 38–39, 45, 65, 85

Suo Otoshi (Dropping the Robe), 32

Terakoya (The Village School), 48, 71, 81, 82, 132
Genba, 48
Genzo, 81
Kan Shusai, 48
Matsuomaru, 71, 82,
Tonami, 81

Tsuchigumo (The Earth Spider), 32, 78, 86, 93

Uiro Uri* (The Uiro Seller), 39

Uwanari* (Jealousy), 39

*Ya no Ne** (The Arrowhead), 39, 94

"Yamabushi Mondo" (Yamabushi Interrogation) from *Kanjincho*, 142–145

Yamanba, 59
    Kaidomaru, 60

Yoshidaya. See *Kuruwa Bunsho*

Yoshitsune Senbon Zakura (Yoshitsune and the Thousand Cherry Trees), 33, 34, 65, 92, 94
    Benkei, 94
    Tadanobu, 92

Yotsuya Kaidan (Ghost Story at Yotsuya), 36, 37–38, 83, 91
    Iemon, 38
    Kohei, 38
    Oiwa, 36, 38, 83

*Zobiki**, 39

Glossary-Index

acrobatics, 18

acting families, most important, 97

acting styles. See *aragoto; wagoto*

actors: adoption of by senior actors, 101; child, 40, 58–60, 97, 121; as directors of plays, 134; generation numbers of, 125; gifts for, 23, 95, 130; names of, 97; school for, 26, 41, 101; students of, 127, 129

agemaku: hanging ringed curtain at the end of the *hanamichi,* 23–24

aibiki: stool to support an actor, 94, 103, 133

akattsura: " red face" character, 47, 48

akutai: speech of abuse, 69-70

anten maku: black curtain dropped to obliterate an entire set, 95

aragoto: bombastic style of acting, 20, 38, 39, 43–45, 70, 83, 84, 92, 99

aramushagoto: "wild warrior style"; full name of *aragoto,* 44

asagi maku: temporary drop-curtain, 95

Asahi Kaisetsu Jigyo, Ltd., 16

audiences: 20; callers in, 125–126; in Kyoto–Osaka region, 46; modern, 21

backstage. See *gakuya*

Buddhist: rosaries, 140, 144, 145; statuary, 44. *See also* Fudo Myoo

bugaku: dances of the imperial court, 17

bukkaeri: on-stage quick change of costume, 31

Bunraku: modern name for Ningyo Joruri puppet theater, 13, 17–18, 19, 32, 33, 34, 35, 76

Bushido: "way of the warrior"; samurai code, 58, 66

butai: stage. See *janome mawashi; mawari-butai*

butai-geiko: stage rehearsal, 132-134

buyo: traditional Japanese dance, 33. *See also* dance

candles, use of, 25, 94

censorship: by Americans, 20-21; by Shogunate, 34

chasen: male wig style, 82

chidori: pattern of *tachimawari* fight scene, 67

Chikamatsu Monzaemon, 18, 19, 35, 131

chikara-gami: stiff paper knot in male wig, symbolizing strength, 43

chisuji no ito: paper spider web thrown by earth spider in *Tsuchigumo,* 93

chukei: old type of fan, 92

chunori: flying, either across the stage or out into the audience, 92

clappers. See *tsuke; ki*

clogs, 43, 65

clowns, 48. See also *sanmaime; doke-gata*

commemoration *kojo.* See *shumei*

costumes. See *isho*

courtesans, 18, 35, 42, 46–47, 65, 82, 83, 93. See also *keisei; oiran*

curtain calls, 153

curtains. See *maku*

daihon: script, 131–132

daimyo: feudal lord, 17

dance: 19, 20, 28–30, 31, 32, 102, 134; and drama in Noh, 17, 31; teachers, 28; traditional, three basic elements of, 29; world of, 32. See also *buyo; nenbutsu odori; ryu*

dance-dramas, 29, 30, 32, 102, 136

danmari: pantomime, 37–38

de-dogu: small props used in a domestic setting, 89, 93

debayashi: nagauta musicians appearing on stage in formal costume, 77

degatari: on-stage appearance of chanter and shamisen player, 77

deha: dance of entry, especially by Sukeroku in the play of the same name, 78

deshi: actor's student, 129

dogu maku: curtain painted to look like a set, 95

doke-gata: clown role, 48

double entrances. See *kari hanamichi*

double suicide. See *shinju*

draw-curtain. See *joshiki maku*

dressing rooms, 82, 101, 127. See also *gakuya*

drop-curtain, 24, 95, 104, 136

drummers in *Kanjincho,* 137, 139, 152

drums. See *taiko*

"Dying Swan," Pavlova's performance of, 73

Earphone Guide, 14, 16, 155, 156–157

ebizori: movement in *tachimawari* fight scene, 67

Edo: former name of Tokyo, 20, 44, 46, 96, 99, 156

Edo period of Japanese history

(1603–1868), 27, 80, 96, 133
Edokko: "sons of Edo," 99
Ejima-Ikushima affair, 96
ennen no mai: "dance of longevity"; final dance section of *Kanjincho,* 72, 152
envoy characters, 81

falsetto: singing, 78; voice used by *onnagata* actors, 41, 42, 69
family crests, 70, 81, 95, 122, 124, 128. See also *mon*
fan clubs, 95, 104, 129. See also *koen kai*
fans, 30, 89, 92, 132, 150; held by singers, 78–79. See also *chukei; mai ogi; uchiwa*
father roles, 57
female-role specialization. See *onnagata*
females on Kabuki stage, 18, 59
feudal lords, 18, 19, 69. *See also* daimyo
floating world. See *ukiyo*
flutes, 17, 75, 77, 136, 137, 141. See also *nohkan; take-bue*
folk dance, 29
Fudo Myoo: Buddhist deity, 44, 140, 142, 143; *mie* performed in the attitude of, 44, 62, 142
Fuji, Mount, 34, 90
furi: movements, especially mime used in dances, 29, 30

gakuya: dressing room, 128–130. *See also* dressing rooms
gakuya Danjuro: minor actor who tries to create a big impression backstage, 129
gakuya suzume: "gakuya sparrow"; fan who is always in the dressing rooms, 129

Garbo, Greta, 13
geisha: female entertainer accomplished in the arts of singing, dancing, the shamisen, and conversation, 82
generation numbers of actors, 125
genkan: vestibule to Japanese room, 128–129
genroku mie: mie named after the Genroku period (1688–1704), 62, 144
geza: off-stage background music, 66, 75–76, 78
ghost plays. See *kaidan-mono*
gidayu: style of chanting and singing used to accompany the puppet theater and some Kabuki plays, 19, 75, 76–77, 78, 79
Ginza: district in Tokyo; location of Kabuki-za, 154
Gion: pleasure quarter in Kyoto, 76
giri: obligation or duty, 35. See also *ninjo*
go-chushin: character who reports on a battle, 92
gojunichi: "fifty-day," male wig, 82
Great Kanto Earthquake, 26
greenroom, 24, 64

habutae: skullcap worn under wig to hold hair in place, 83–84
Hachiman: god of war, 147
haiku: three-line poem of seventeen syllables, 68
hakama: pleated trousers or culottes (for men), 81. See also *naga-bakama*

hana: "flower"; reference to a gift to actor, 23

hana yoten: group of men who attack the hero in *tachimawari* stage-fight, 67

hanamichi: walkway extension to the main stage, 15, 22–24, 25, 26, 72, 153, 155. See also *kari hanamichi*

harakiri. See *seppuku*

hashigakari: hanamichi of the Noh stage, 23, 24

hashiramaki no mie: mie pose in which the actor wraps one arm and one leg around a pillar, 62

Heian period of Japanese history (794–1185), 17, 33

Heike Monogatari (The Tale of the Heike), 33

Heike-Genji civil wars, 33, 136

hengemono: "transformation pieces"; sequence of dances involving quick costume changes, 30

hibachi: charcoal brazier, 93

hikimaku: draw-curtain, 22. See also *joshiki maku*

hikinuki: quick, on-stage change technique in which a kimono held together by threads is pulled off the actor to reveal a different kimono underneath, 30–31, 102

hime-sama: princess role, 41–42

history plays. See *jidaimono*

Hogan Dono: formal title of Yoritomo's half-brother Yoshitsune, 145

home kotoba: "words of praise"; early tradition of interrupting a play to allow a fan to praise an actor; forerunner of *kakegoe,* 125

homosexuality, 19

honchoshi: one of the three tunings of the shamisen, 75

hyogo mage: courtesan's wig, 83

hyoshigi: wooden clappers used for *ki* or *tsuke* beats, 63. See also *ki; tsuke*

Ichikawa acting family, 44, 70, 97, 124

Ichimura-za: one of the three great theaters of Edo, 25, 26

Ichiriki-ya: teahouse in Gion, Kyoto, 76

ie no gei: "family art"; acting traditions handed down within an acting family, 38, 44

imo arai: "potato washing"; severed heads stirred around in a barrel, 94

ishinage no mie: mie performed with one arm raised as if throwing a stone, 62, 150

isho: costumes: 32, 35, 71, 80–81, 129; for *chunori,* 92; family crests on, 122, 124; quick changes of, 30–31, 102; in rehearsals, 132; restrictions on, 96

ito ni noru: "riding the strings"; the actor times his speech and movements to the rhythm of the shamisen, 68

janome mawashi: revolving inner stage, now obsolete, 26. See also *mawari-butai*

jidai danmari, 37. See also *danmari; sewa danmari*

jidaimono: "history plays" set in Japan's real or legendary past, 20, 28, 32–35, 37, 61, 68

jitsu-aku: male role type, the evil samurai, 47, 48, 57

joshiki maku: striped draw-curtain used in all Kabuki theaters, 24–25, 95

Juhachiban: collection of eighteen plays of the Ichikawa Danjuro line of actors, 38–39, 44, 70, 100, 124

Kabuki, meaning of word, 19–20. See also *kabuku*

Kabuki *odori:* early Kabuki dances, 28

Kabuki-za: Kabuki theater in Tokyo, 16, 22, 128, 132, 154–155, 157; destruction and rebuilding of, 21, 26

kabuku: archaic verb meaning tilted or strange; origin of the word "Kabuki," 18

kaidan-mono: ghost plays, 36, 83, 91

kaishaku: assistant in a *seppuku*, 58

kakegoe: skillfully timed calls of appreciation made by the audience, 14, 63, 73, 124–126, 130, 137, 141, 153, 155

Kamakura period of Japanese history (1185–1336), 33

kamishimo: ceremonial dress of the samurai, also worn by onstage musicians, 81, 102, 103, 124

Kamo River, Kyoto: site of earliest Kabuki performances, 18, 96

Kanamaru-za: Edo-period theater still in use in Shikoku, 27

Kannami: one of the founders of Noh theater, 29

kaomise: "face showing"; the start of the Kabuki new year, when new actors are introduced to the audience, 37, 48

kari hanamichi: temporary *hanamichi*, 26

kasumi maku: curtain used to hide musicians before they are required to play, 95

kata: forms or models defining the way actors perform certain roles, 36, 71–73, 134

kataginu: shoulder wings of the *kamishimo* costume, 81

katahazushi: female wig style, 83

kataki-yaku: evil male role, 47

kato bushi: musical style, 78

katsura: wig, 82. *See also* wigs

kawaramono: "object of the riverbed"; early derogatory name for Kabuki actors, 96

Kawarazaki-za: theater in Edo, 38

Kawatake Mokuami, 25, 131

keisei: courtesans, 46–47. *See also* courtesans; *oiran*

keisei roppo: courtesan's exit, 65

keisei-kai: "courtesan buying"; the process of obtaining the favors of a courtesan, 47

keshi maku: hand-held curtain used to hide an actor either before a dramatic appearance or after the death of a character, 95

kesho: makeup, 83. *See also* makeup

ki: clappers most commonly

used to signal the start and end of a play, 63, 64, 152

kiemono: hand props that are destroyed in the course of a performance, 93

kimari: softer version of the *mie,* performed by female characters, 62

kimono: definition of, 80; family crest on, 124; of premodern Japan, 30; in quick costume changes, 31, 102; of samurai's wife, 81; sleeves of, 30, 80

Kinpira: Edo-period puppet character, 44

kirido-guchi: small door set in Noh stage for rapid entrances and exits; seen in Kabuki *matsubame-mono,* 31

kiseru: pipe, 93

kitsune roppo: "fox exit," 65

kiyomoto: lyrical music style, 78–79

Kiyomoto Enjudayu: founder of *kiyomoto* music style, 78

Kiyomoto Shizudayu: *kiyomoto* singer, 78

ko-dogu: small props, 89, 92–93

koen kai: actor's fan club, 104. *See also* fan clubs

kojo: formal stage announcement, 98, 104, 121–122, 124

koken: formally dressed stage assistant, 102–103, 124

Kokugikan: Tokyo sumo stadium, 26

kokumochi: single-color kimono of the wife of a samurai, 81

Kokuritsu Gekijo. *See* National Theater of Japan

Korai-ya: *yago* of the Matsumoto acting line, 98

ko-tsuzumi: hand drum played at the shoulder, 75, 77

koyaku: child roles, 40, 58–60, 121

kubi jikken: inspection to identify a severed head, 94

kuge-aku: evil aristocrat, male-role type, 47, 48, 57

kumadori: stylized makeup designs, 44, 47, 48, 83–86

kumo-te tako-ashi roppo: "spider hands and octopus leg" exit, 65

kuriage: vocal technique used when characters argue, 69

kurogo: black-dressed stage assistant, 59, 94, 102, 103

Kyogen: comedies performed with Noh plays, 17, 19

Kyoto: modern Kabuki theater in, 48, 156; origin of Kabuki in, 18, 96; and *wagoto* acting style, 43, 45–46;

Kyoto-Osaka region: audiences, 46; origin of *sewamono* in, 35; star actors in, 96

lifts: in *hanamichi,* 24; in stage, 90

lighting, 25, 26, 83, 134

lion dances, 78, 102

Living National Treasure: title of honor bestowed by the Japanese government, 103, 127

ma: pregnant pause in speech or movement, 125, 126

machi musume: town girl, 41

mai: old term for dance; slow and stately dancing, 29

mai ogi: dance fan, 92

makeup, 43, 44, 48, 71, 83–88, 103. See also *kesho; kumadori*

maku: curtains, 22, 23–25, 95. See

also *agemaku; anten maku; dogu maku;* drop-curtain; *joshiki maku; kasumi maku; keshi maku*

maku mi: fourth floor of the Kabuki-za, where one may see only one act of a play, 155

male-role specialization, 40. See also *tachiyaku*

masks in Noh theater, 17

masu: tatami-mat box seats used in theaters before the advent of Western-style seating, 26

matsubame-mono: plays derived from the Noh theater, 31, 32

Matsushima-ya: *yago* of the Kataoka acting line, 135, 147

mawari-butai: revolving stage, 25–26, 90–91, 156

Meiji era of Japanese history (1868–1912), 26, 42

Meiji restoration, 96, 100

michiyuki: "travel-dance," often depicting a couple traveling to commit double suicide. *See* travel-dance

mie: stylized stop-motion pose, 37, 44, 45, 61–63, 64, 72, 121, 125, 126, 153. See also *kimari*

mime: 19, 30, 66, 150, 152. See also *furi*

Minami-za: theater in Kyoto, 48, 156

Minamoto Yoritomo: Shogun, elder half-brother of Yoshitsune; leader of the Genji clan, 136, 137, 139

Minamoto Yoshitsune: younger half-brother of Yoritomo; heroic figure in many Kabuki plays, 33, 136

Misono-za: theater in Nagoya, 156

modern plays: 20, 74

mon: actors' family crests, 122, 124. *See also* family crests

Morita-za: one of the three great theaters of Edo, 25, 26

mukimi-guma: kumadori makeup style, 85

murasaki boshi: purple patch of silk on the front of a female wig, 82

music: 25, 28, 74–79, 137; stands for, 79. See also *geza; nagauta*

musicians: 31, 32, 74–75, 77, 79, 132, 136, 141; costumes of, 81

naga-bakama: long *hakama*, 43, 81. See also *hakama*

nagauta: "long song"; principal musical style of Kabuki, 77–78, 79, 136

Nagoya, modern theater in, 156

Nagoya Sanza: famous samurai depicted in Okuni's Kabuki, 18

Naka-za: theater in Osaka, 156

Nakamura-ya: *yago* of the Nakamura Kanzaburo line of actors, 135, 137

Nakamura-za: one of the three great theaters of Edo, 25, 26

names of actors, 97

name-saying speech. See *tsurane*

nami no oto: "wave sounds"; musical sound effect, 76

Namiki Shozo: credited with the invention of the revolving stage, 25

Nanzenji: temple in Kyoto, 90

Narita, temple in, 99, 125

Narita-ya: *yago* of the Ichikawa Danjuro line of actors, 99, 125, 135

National Theater of Japan, 22, 26, 154, 155–156, 157; revivals of plays by, 39, 132

National Theater Kabuki School, 26, 41, 101

nenbutsu odori: old ceremonial religious dance, 18, 29

niagari: one of the tunings of the shamisen, 75

nihon suji-guma: kumadori makeup style, 85

nimaime: "second flat thing"; young male role, 48

Ningyo Joruri: puppet theater now called Bunraku, 17. *See also* Bunraku

ninjo: emotion; human feeling, 35. See also *giri*

nirami: glaring, especially a cross-eyed *mie* pose, 121

Noh: 13, 17, 18, 19, 29, 31, 32, 100, 136, 137, 139, 152; stage, 17, 18, 22, 23, 24, 25; theater, 25

nohkan: flute used in the Noh theater, 75, 77

noren: hanging curtain used in a doorway, 128

nuigurumi: animal costumes, 93–94

obi: kimono sash, 80, 81

o-dachi: "great sword," used by Kamakura Gongoro in *Shibaraku,* 92–93

o-daiko: large drum, 75, 76

o-dogu: stage sets, 89–92. *See also* sets

odori: dance. See *buyo;* dance; *furi; mai*

ohaguro: substance used by married women to blacken their teeth, 84

ohayo gozaimasu (Good morning): first greeting of the day in the Kabuki world, 129, 133

oiran: courtesans, also called *keisei,* 42, 46–47. *See also* courtesans

Oishi Kuranosuke: real-life hero of the *Kanadehon Chushingura* story, 34

Okuni: female dancer who founded Kabuki, 18, 40

Omodaka-ya: *yago* of the Ichikawa Ennosuke acting line, 125

o-muko-san: "professional" members of the audience who perform *kakegoe,* 126

onnagata: male player of female roles, 13, 19, 30, 40, 41–42, 69, 121, 138

Onoe Kikugoro acting line, 71, 125

onryogoto: "resentful spirit plays," 30

opera: Chinese, 84; Western, 14

Osaka, 46; modern theaters in, 156; puppet theater in, 18. *See also* Kyoto–Osaka region

oshiguma: face pressing; silk pressed onto makeup, 86–88, 127, 129, 130

oshiroi: white cream base makeup, 84

otokogata: old term for a male-role player, now *tachiyaku,* 41

Otowa-ya: *yago* of the Onoe acting family, 71, 125, 135, 137

otsukare sama (You must be very tired!): final greeting of the day in the Kabuki world, 130

o-tsuzumi: side drum played with thimbles on the fingers, 75, 77, 140 pantomime. See *danmari*

paper wad used as prop, 93

Pavlova, Anna, 73

percussion instruments, 75

pipes. See *kiseru*

pitch of actors' voices, 69

playwrights, 18, 19, 20, 25, 35, 131

poetry. *See* haiku; *shichi-go-cho*

princess roles. See *hime-sama; shibire hime*

props. See *de-dogu; kiemono; ko-dogu*

proscenium arch, 23, 25

prostitution, 18, 19, 46

puppet, imitation of, 102

puppet theater. *See* Bunraku; Ningyo Joruri

rehearsals, 131–134. See also *butai geiko*

religious dances. See *nenbutsu odori*

revolving stage. See *mawari-butai; janome mawashi*

roppo: vigorous stylized exit on the *hanamichi*, 64–66, 153. See also *keisei roppo; kitsune roppo; kumo-te tako-ashi roppo; tanzen roppo; tobi roppo*

ryu: guild or school, usually of dance, 32

samurai: warrior class of feudal Japan, 17, 18; costume of, 81; forty-seven, 34; portrayal of, 32, 47, 48; ritual suicide of, 57–58; swords, 92

sandan: three steps leading from the stage up to a building, 90

sangai yakusha: "third-floor actor," who plays minor role, 101, 128

sanmaime: clown role, 48. See also *doke-gata*

sanri-ate: pads tied beneath the knees to cover points used for moxibustion treatment, 81

sansagari: one of the tunings of the shamisen, 75

sashidashi: candles held on long poles to illuminate an actor, 94

scripts. See *daihon*

seating, theater, 26

sekai: "world"; a number of plays set in a particular era or about a particular subject, 33

senshuraku: last day of a Kabuki run, 132

seppuku: ritual suicide by disembowelment; also called *hara-kiri*, 34, 37, 57–58

serifu: speech, 67–70. See also *wari-zerifu; watari-zerifu*

sets: 31, 32, 35, 71, 89–92

severed heads, 94

sewa danmari: domestic pantomime, 37

sewamono: plays of the common people, depicting life in feudal Japan, 20, 28, 35–37, 57, 61, 67–68, 80

shamisen: three-stringed lutelike instrument, 18, 68, 75, 76, 140; tuning of, 75; used in *gidayu*, 77

shibire hime: "pins and needles princess," 42

shichi-go-cho: 7-5 syllabic meter in Japanese poetry, 68

shichi-san: "seven-three" position on the *hanamichi*, 24

shikimi: Japanese anise plant, used in *seppuku*, 57

Shikoku, Edo-period theater in, 27

Shimbashi Embujo: theater in Tokyo, 156

Shin Kabuki-za: theater in Osaka, 156

shinju: lovers' double suicide, 36, 47

shiranami-mono: "white wave plays," about thieves, 36

Shochiku Co. Ltd., 16

Shogun: military governor, 18, 136

Shogunate: military government, 18, 34, 46, 66; regulation of Kabuki by, 19, 20, 82, 96

shonichi: first day of a Kabuki run, 132

shosa-butai: special smooth surface laid onto the main stage for dancing, 29

shosagoto: dance plays, 20, 28

shumei: name-taking ceremony, 95, 97–99, 101, 103, 121, 135

shumei kojo: formal stage announcement that an actor is taking a new name, 121

singers: 31, 75, 77, 137, 145, 151, 152

Soga Monogatari (The Tale of the Soga Brothers), 33

sound effects, 76

souvenirs for the audience, 124

speech. See *serifu*

stage assistants. See *koken; kurogo*

stage names, 97

students of actors. See *deshi*

stylization: of acting, 42, 61; of posing, 36; of speech, 67. See also *tachimawari*

suicide. See *seppuku; shinju*

supernatural appearances, 24

suppon: lift in the *hanamichi*, 24

suri-ashi: heel-to-the-ground sliding step common in Noh theater, 29, 32

swords, 63, 66, 92. See also *o-dachi*

symbols: of illness, 47; of strength, 43

tachimawari: stylized fight scenes, 63, 66–67, 133

tachiyaku: male-role actor, 40, 41, 43

taiko: drum, 75, 77, 102. See also *ko-tsuzumi; o-daiko*

Takashima-ya: *yago* of Ichikawa Sadanji line of actors, 135

take-bue: bamboo flute, 75, 77

Takemoto Gidayu: founder of Gidayu style of narration and musical accompaniment first used to accompany the puppet theater, 18, 19, 76

tanzen roppo: stylized walk popular with the dandies of Edo, adopted by Kabuki actors, 65

tatami: thick reed matting, 26

tateshi: tachimawari fight choreographer, 67

Tenchijin Mie, 141–142

tenugui: hand towel often used as hand prop in dance, 30, 124

theaters: early, 19, 24; Edo, 25, 26; lighting of, 26, 83, 94; managers of, 99; seating in, 26; Western-style, 24, 26

ticket prices, 155, 156

tobi roppo: flying or bounding exit, 25, 45, 63, 64, 153

Todaiji: temple in Nara, 139

Tokiwazu Mojidayu: founder of *tokiwazu* music style, 78

tokiwazu: music style, 78, 79

toko-yama: craftsmen who dress Kabuki wigs, 81–82, 129

Tokyo: and Danjuro, 99; former name of, 20; theaters in, 22, 25, 26, 128, 154–156. *See also* Edo

tonbo: somersault symbolizing a kill in a *tachimawari* fight, 66

travel-dance, 67, 90

tsuke: wooden clappers used to accompany *mie* poses and for sound effects, 62, 63–64, 66, 72, 121–122, 150

tsuke uchi: man who beats the *tsuke* clappers, 63, 64

tsukebito: actor's backstage assistant, 129

tsurane: formal "name-saying" speech in which an actor introduces himself and his character to the other on-stage characters and to the audience, 69, 70, 102

Tsuruya Nanboku: playwright, 25, 131

uchiwa: nonfolding flat fan, 92

ukiyo: the "floating world" of the pleasure quarters—of teahouses and theaters, 19

ukiyo-e: pictures of the "floating world"; woodblock prints depicting the world of pleasures—beautiful women, Kabuki actors, and love-making, 19

uma no shippo: "pony tail"; female wig, 83

umbrellas, 93

villains. See *kataki-yaku*

vocal delivery, 43, 44, 46, 67, 71, 84

wagoto: soft or gentle style of acting, 20, 35, 43, 45–47, 48

wakashu Kabuki: Kabuki performed by young boys between 1629 and 1652, 18

wari-zerifu: speech divided between two characters, 69

watari-zerifu: speech passed along a line of characters, 69

wigs, 43, 46, 47, 48, 81–83, 103, 104, 121, 129. See also *chasen; gojunichi; hyogo mage; katahazushi; uma no shippo*

wigmaker. See *toko-yama*

World War II: censorship following, 20; firebombing during, 26

yago: acting-house name of an actor; name associated with an actor's acting family tradition, 71, 97, 98, 99, 125, 135, 141

yamabushi: sect of wandering warrior priests, 136, 142

yamagata: "mountain shape" formed by swords in *tachimawari* fight scene, 67

Yamato-ya: *yago* of the majority of the Bando family of actors, 135

yaro Kabuki: mature male Kabuki, the forerunner of present-day Kabuki, 19

Yashima: site of one of the great battles in which Yoshitsune defeated the Heike clan, 150

yukata: light, summer kimono, 132

Zeami: one of the founders of
the Noh theater, 29

OTHER TERMS:

Readers may find the following terms in other works about Kabuki:

akahime: "red princess"; upper-class young girl dressed in scarlet
kimono
ame no oto: "sound of rain" musical sound effect
bata-bata, ba-tan: onomatopoeic words for the striking of the *tsuke* wood
blocks
beni: rouge makeup
bokashi: smudging of lines of color in *kumadori* makeup
chaya: teahouse; place of assignation
chobo: the *gidayu* chanter and shamisen player
chon mage: the samurai topknot
chonin: commoners, below the rank of samurai
daigane: copper mold of the actor's head onto which the wig hair is
sown
daimon: "great crest"; male costume decorated with the family crest of
the character
eboshi: conical hat worn by men and sometimes women, as by Hanako
in *Musume Dojoji*
Genji: one of the two principal clans in the Heike-Genji civil wars
geta: wooden clogs
haiyu: modern Japanese word for "actor." See also *yakusha*
haori: three-quarter-length garment or outer coat worn by men and
women over the kimono
hayagawari: quick change of costume
Heike: one of the two principal clans in the Heike-Genji civil wars
hippari no mie: mie pose expressing tension between two or more
characters
iemoto: head of a school of dance, Noh, tea ceremony, or other
traditional art
ippon-guma: style of *kumadori* makeup
janome-gasa: umbrella with bull's-eye design, as used by Sukeroku in
the play of the same name
jitte: hand-weapon carried by Kabuki policemen
joruri: music based on narration with shamisen accompaniment,
usually called *gidayu*

kagura: Shinto dance and music

kaishi: wad of tissue paper carried in the breast of the kimono

kamiko: kimono originally made of paper; worn by Izaemon in *Kuruwa Bunsho*

kanzashi: long, ornate hairpin

katana: sword

katsureki-geki: "living history plays," written for Ichikawa Danjuro IX

kaze no oto: "sound of wind" musical sound effect

kesho goe: on-stage chant of the meaningless phrase "Ariya, Koriya!" by minor characters used to provide an imposing aural background for a main character

kido: small gate incorporated into the set

kokyu: bowed string instrument from China

komuso: wandering sect of priests who covered their faces with large sedge hats and played the *shakuhachi* bamboo flute

kuchibeni: lip rouge

kudoki: scene in which a woman displays her emotions

kuruma-bin: stylized *aragoto* wig, worn by Kamakura Gongoro in *Shibaraku*

mage: topknot section of a wig

monogatari: section of a play in which the main character tells the story of a battle or other event

naraku: "hell"; the area backstage under the *hanamichi*

ningyo: doll; puppet

onna Kabuki: women's Kabuki, the earliest form of Kabuki, founded by Okuni

otokodate: chivalrous commoner, below samurai class

ronin: "wave men"; masterless samurai

ryujin maki: stylized costume of an envoy, as worn by Seno in *Shunkan*

saru guma: "monkey" *kuma*, oldest of *kumadori* makeup styles

sensu: fans

seri: lift set into the stage

Shin Juhachiban: "New Juhachiban," a collection of plays made by Danjuro VIII and IX

shirabyoshi: female dancing entertainer, as Hanako in *Musume Dojoji*

sode: sleeve of kimono

suji kuma: line makeup serving as foundation for *kumadori*

suo: formal outer robe worn by men

tabi: socks with separate section for the big toe

tachi mi: "standing room only" in the Kabuki theater

Takemoto-za: puppet theater founded by Takemoto Gidayu

toya: greenroom at the end of the *hanamichi*

tsuri eda: sprigs of cherry blossom decoration hanging above the stage set

uchikake: woman's ceremonial outer robe

uta: "song"; the character for the word can also be read as "ka," hence the first syllable of "Kabuki"

yagura: a drum tower erected outside the theater as a symbol of the license to perform granted by the government

yakusha: traditional Japanese word for actor

Yoshiwara: the pleasure quarter of Edo

zori: straw sandals